Connectio

A Spiritual Memoir and Yoga Journey

By Susan Rosler

Table of Contents

Dedication

I'd like to dedicate this book to all our loved ones, especially those spirits in the atmosphere that show up, when we are paying attention, to make us smile.

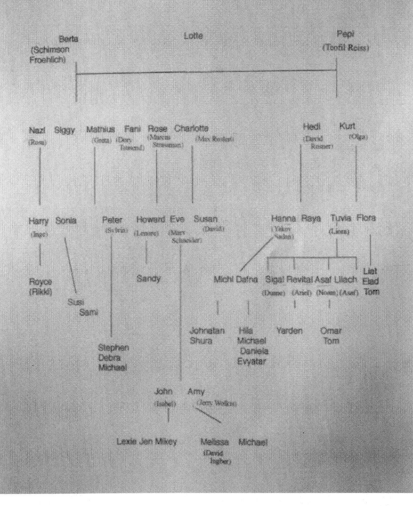

Hersch

Berta
(Schimson
Froehlich)

Lotte

Pepi
(Teofil Reiss)

Nazi
(Rosa)

Siggy

Mathius
(Greta)

Fani
(Dory
Tausend)

Rose
(Marcus
Strassman)

Charlotte
(Max Roxler)

Hedi
(David
Rosner)

Kurt
(Olga)

Harry
(Inge)

Sonia

Peter
(Sylvia)

Howard
(Lenore)

Eve
(Marv
Schneider)

Susan
(David)

Hanna
(Yakov
Sadan)

Raya

Tuvia
(Liora)

Flora

Royce
(Rikki)

Sandy

Susi
Sami

Michi Dafna

Sigal Revital Asaf Lilach
(Duane) (Ariel) (Noam) (Asaf)

List
Elad
Tom

Stephen
Debra
Michael

Johnatan
Shura

Hila
Michael
Daniela
Evyatar

Yarden

Omar
Tom

John
(Isabel)

Amy
(Jerry Welkos)

Lexie Jen Mikey

Melissa
(David
Ingber)

Michael

5

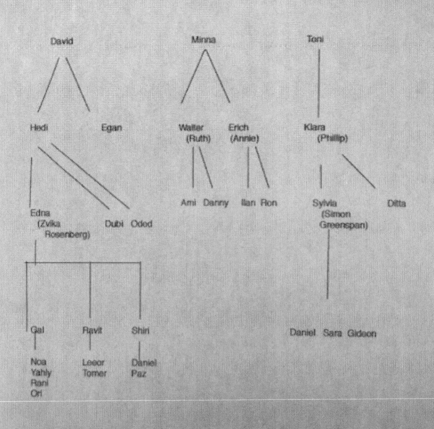

Jochewed

David   Minna   Toni

Hedi   Egan   Walter   Erich   Klara
               (Ruth) (Annie) (Phillip)

                        Ami Danny Ilan Ron   Sylvia   Ditta
Edna   (Simon
(Zvika   Dubi Oded   Greenspan)
Rosenberg)

Gal   Ravit   Shiri   Daniel Sara Gideon

Noa   Leeor Daniel
Yahly Tomer Paz
Rani
Ori

6

Kamil family photo, 1912

My Maternal Great Grandparents, Hersch and Jochewed Kamil

Counter clockwise from left - My Great Grandfather (Hersch), Nazl, Berta, Siggy (baby), Great Grandmother (Jochewed), Toni, Minna, David, Pepi, my Grandfather (Schimson), Lotte

1 **MAGGIE**, Life Is Eternal

My best friend, Maggie, was a knockout. There she stood, smiling and joking, entertaining a circle of admirers. Her classy Manhattan apartment had natural wood floors that were warmed with thick, genuine, beige tone Persian rugs. The spacious apartment served as a perfect backdrop for the generous parties that she often hosted.

Maggie was a raven haired, dark eyed, olive skinned Sephardic beauty with straight posture and a form that was sculpted and fit as she held court, hand on hip, delivering that famous Mae West line, "Is that a pistol in your pocket or are you just happy to see me?" She displayed the full spectrum of comedy, heart, and sex appeal by her rich infectious laugh that resounded regularly wherever she went. A crisp, white, short-sleeved blouse with shoulder pads and frilly lace at the neck, and a black silky pencil skirt showcased her magnificent form. Her legs always sparkled in high heels, short skirts or shorts with shapely calf muscles developed by her disciplined early morning runs.

One evening, sporting her red shiny stiletto heeled shoes, her chic purse swinging from her shoulder, she strutted down 83rd Street when suddenly her purse was snatched by a brazen young man. Having astute reflexes, she instantaneously took off her shoes and flew after him. Eliciting the help of a stranger, she tackled him to the ground and belted him with her sharp shoes and metallic purse. The unsuspecting mugger never had a chance. That was Maggie.

One lovely afternoon, she suggested a museum outing. I came by and she took me to her favorite neighbor deli. She negotiated with the man for a half-pound of roast beef, sliced fine and very lean...very lean. She then orchestrated the preparation of the sandwiches: roast beef, lettuce, mustard and several slices of hand-picked juicy red tomato and the slices, thick cut...but just a fraction more. All this arranged on fresh-seeded rye bread.

The day was exciting and filled with laughter. Thinking back, I can't remember what made it so special. Was it the museum exhibit? No-o, don't remember that...or the roast beef? Or was it the tomato? No, it was Maggie.

Maggie, died of Leukemia. Before her illness, she was an acquaintance among a group of friends. After a bone marrow transplant and heavy chemotherapy, she was very near the end, but managed to survive. As a result, she didn't want to deal with the other superficial ladies and we became very close.

Maggie was the most loyal and the truest friend imaginable. She was always there. Part of a large family, with several sisters and brothers, she had many nieces and nephews. Being sincere, pure and dynamic, she was everyone's favorite aunt. One day Maggie and her cousin Ida decided to fix me up with Ida's old boy friend, David.

Keeping a long-term relationship was always difficult for me. I needed to have a partner or even a team of experts in order to stay involved. David and I became an item after the first date. Our personalities and gifts complemented each other, but we argued a lot. Sometimes phone conversations led to disputes and David, not knowing what to do, would hang up. I, not knowing what to do, would call Maggie.

She would say, "Just a minute," put me on hold, and called Ida.

Ida said, "Just a minute" and called David.

David then called me and I, relieved, told Maggie, "Just a minute, the other phone, it's David."

Eventually David and I were married. Maggie continued to be there for us.

Alas, during the fifth year of her survival, she began a downhill spiral. In September, I went to visit her in Seattle, Washington, where she was in the hospital for treatment.

I returned home and sent her a card. Shortly afterwards, she went to L.A. to stay with her brother and family. We were on the phone steadily. On her last day, I called. The family was gathered round her bedside. They put the phone to her ear and I told her how much I loved her. This was in November. March 25 was my birthday. I returned from work feeling lonely on this, my special day. I opened the mailbox and there was a card in a red envelope with Maggie's name on it. Astonished, I rushed upstairs and opened it. It read, "I want to let you know that I love you." I pondered and finally figured it out.

This was the card that I had sent her in September at the hospital. She left and never received it. It must have been lost in the mail for six months and finally was 'returned to sender' exactly on my birthday, four months after her passing. I cried tears of joy knowing that I had evidence that her spirit was alive and still with me: an angel that I could call upon when I needed her. I thanked her for her message, kindness, devotion and strength.

My dog and David's companion, Letterman, was Maggie's favorite "nephew". Letterman understood, comforted me and licked my tears. He too, remembered Maggie.

9

Maggie

2 **GLADYS,** "Find Those Great Nieces"

Gladys said, "Generations are going by, find those great nieces."
I followed up by daring to ask Melissa, my great niece, for the emails of Jen and Lexie, my nephews children. What would I say to them after all these years? I saw them in their tree house when they were 5 and 7, and on opposite ends of the dinner table at 16 and 18. Just in time, came an email from cousin Tuvia, in Israel, with a beautiful article he had written about his mother, Olga.

Susan and Gladys

counterclockwise - Isabel (John's wife) , Lexie, Mikey (youngest), Melissa (Amy's daughter), Jen, Jerry (Amy's husband), Amy, Eve, David (Melissa's husband) and John, my nephew

3 **OLGA** "Mamma" by Tuvia Erez, The Power of Song

On April 16, 2015, Susan Rosler wrote:

Hi Lexie and Jen,
Wanted to say hello and connect. I am attaching an article written by cousin
Tuvia in Israel about his mom, Olga, a concentration camp survivor. We have a
fascinating heritage.
Love, Aunt Susan

My mother's cousin Kurt and his wife Olga

MAMMA

By Tuvia (Toby) Erez (Reiss)

This short article that Tuvia wrote is his loving tribute to his mother, Olga, a holocaust survivor, who passed away a few years ago. This story was published in his home town newspaper shortly after her death. He would like to share it with all of us in honor of Holocaust Remembrance Day.
****

43177. That's the number the Germans branded on my mother's left arm when she arrived in Auschwitz. In 1943, dark clouds covered the bright blue skies of Thessaloniki, Greece. Seventeen year-old Olga and her family were taken to a concentration camp. When the war ended, my mother found her way to Belgium, where she was taken in by a family of Righteous Gentiles, and then to Israel. The war was over, but the clouds that covered the bright blue skies remained and covered my mother's life in a permanent grey hue; the color of the smoky chimneys from which her loved ones perished. From time to time, a ray of light beckoned in the form of the birth of children, grandchildren, and her great-granddaughter Tamar. But over the years, as I looked into my mother's eyes, I would always see the 17-year-old girl whose life stood still in Auschwitz, in 1943.

Two years ago, when that damn disease that got her had only begun, she called me one morning. "Have I ever told you," she asked, "how I survived the concentration camp?" "No, Mother," I said, "you've never told me."
"Would you like me to tell you?" she asked.
"Of course," I said. And she began to talk.
"The German officers guarding the concentration camp loved Neapolitan songs. One day they came to us, the prisoners, and asked, 'Is there anyone here who can sing the song MAMMA by the famous Italian tenor Beniamino Gigli?'"
"I knew the song," she continued, "because my father, who loved Neapolitan songs, used to sing it to us often. So I sang it in front of the German officers. I must have sung it well because from that day, every time they wanted to hear

the song they called for me and said, 'Greeka (the Greek woman), sing MAMMA for us.' And I sang because my life depended on it. That's how I was saved."

"Would you like me to sing you the song?" she continued to ask me on the other end of the line. "Of course, Mother," I replied. She began singing into the receiver MAMMA in Italian, and I on the other end wiped a tear.

My mother never returned to Thessaloniki. The memories were too painful. A few years back, I told her I was going on a trip to Northern Greece and Thessaloniki and asked her to write down the address where she had lived. She remembered the street name: Edmond Rostand (the name of a French author). She did not remember the house number, but said that across the street was a synagogue with the Hebrew words "Gifts for the Poor" inscribed on its front.

On a spring day we arrived in Thessaloniki. We found the street immediately - a long straight road in the middle of town. The houses were typical to Greece: each house five stories, painted white, with a meter-wide balcony surrounding each floor. On the balconies, the inhabitants sat on chairs facing the street, and watched the passersby. We began walking along the street and approached passersby, asking them where we could find the synagogue. No one knew. And then we saw him - an old Greek man at an age likely to have been touched by war in youth. We approached him, but he did not speak any English - only Greek and German. We began to converse with simultaneous translations, telling him who we were and what we were after.

The Greek told us that during the war he was a boy, maybe 10. He didn't know where there a synagogue was in the area, but said he had a friend who was one of the leaders of the Jewish community in Thessaloniki, and suggested she might be able to help.

Following him, we walked to one of the side streets and reached an extravagant house with multiple floors. The Greek pushed the intercom button, said a few words and the door opened. Receiving us at the door was a woman dressed in black. Her apartment was extremely well maintained and pristinely clean; pictures of her son (so she said) at various Maccabiah sport competitions were scattered along the walls. Soon, however, we found ourselves yet again in a dead-end conversation. The woman spoke only Ladino and Greek, the man spoke only Greek and German, and we knew only German and Hebrew. Words and questions were lost along the way. Eventually, I took out my cell phone and called my mother in Tel Aviv. "Mom," I spoke in Hebrew of course, "there's a woman here who speaks Ladino - explain to her what we're looking for." I passed the phone to the woman in black and she spoke to my mother in Ladino. I did not understand a word, because growing up we spoke only Hebrew and German in our house, but the sound of the words enveloped me like the warmth of my mother's home. After they finished speaking, she gestured with her hand, and we followed her as she walked down the street.

After a 20-minute walk, we arrived at a small, preserved house, surrounded by a fine fence. There was a guard-booth at the entrance. We went around the house to the back. On the white wall, large metal letters spelled "Gifts for the Poor." I had come full circle.

To my mother, who passed this year, I dedicate the song that saved her life at the camp, "MAMMA". (Below)

MAMMA / Beniamino Gigli

Mamma, I'm so happy because I return to you.
My song tells you. It's the most beautiful dream for me!
Mamma I'm so happy. Why should one live so far away?
Mamma, just only for you my song is flying.
Mamma, you will be with me, you will not be alone anymore!
How much I love you!
These words of love, sighed for you by my heart,
maybe are not used anymore.
Mamma! But my most beautiful song is you!
It is you for a lifetime (you are my life).
And in my life I will not leave you again!
I feel your tired hand. It's searching for my golden curls.
I feel it, and your voice is feeble, the lullaby - that old lullaby - you used to sing back then (back to the past).
Today your head is whitening. I want to hold it close to my heart.
Mamma
You are my most beautiful song
You are my life
And I will not leave you anymore in my life!

Tuvia and his wife Liora with Susan

Tuvia is the son of Kurt and Olga. Olga was Greek. Kurt was my mother's first cousin.

On Apr 21, 2015, at 9:09 PM, Jen Schneider wrote:

Hey Aunt Susan,
   I read the story and could not believe how interesting it was. Hope all is well with you!!
Xoxo jen and lexie

Hi Girls,
   Olga and I met in 1967 when I first visited Israel after the "67" war. She was extremely beautiful and very gracious. She and her husband, cousin Kurt, invited me to stay at their apartment in Tel Aviv. Since the place was small, the children, Tuvia and Flora, slept elsewhere, with their friends. Last summer (2014) I had the opportunity to visit Tuvia, who I not seen, would you believe, since that year. David and I stayed in the guest room. The visit was exciting. Tuvia and I would talk late at night exchanging stories of the relatives. He showed me two published books and gave me a copy of one of them. It was the memoirs of his father with photos of the family in Vienna before they left. I recognized my mother with her sisters, brothers and parents.
   Love, Susan

4 **EMAILS TO THE GIRLS** Fishing for a Hook,
Viennese Cremeschnitt by Tuvia Erez

On *Apr 22, 2015, at 2:19 PM, Alexis Schneider wrote:*

Hello Aunt Susan,

It is great to hear from you it has been too long. This is extremely interesting, we definitely do have a very fascinating heritage and it is very sad that I don't know much about it, I love learning this stuff please continue to keep in touch. If you could please let me know the names of these books that would be great! Look forward to hearing from you!   Love, Lexie

Hi Girls,

I looked on the internet but couldn't find them. One is written in Hebrew and the other in German and translated to Hebrew. They are self-published by the family members, not easy to track down.
Will send other information as ideas come to me.

Lovingly, Aunt Susan

On Apr 22, 2015, Jen Schneider wrote

Thank you for looking for the books! If you had any old photos we would Love to see them!!!!

Oxoxoxo jen

Hi Girls,

I will get back to the story in a month or so after my trip. Presently I am getting ready for the cousins' reunion in Vienna, starting on June 9.

Three cousins and their spouses from Israel will be there. But also, as special guest, will be my first cousin, Peter Froehlich, who was born and raised in England after his father, Mathias, my mother's brother, escaped from Vienna.

Counterclockwise from left: Rose, Fani, Mathius, My Grandfather (Schimson), Siggy, My Grandmother (Berta), Nazl. My mother was not yet born.

Froehlich Family Photo/Mathius is the youngest in the center

Hope you are interested in all this, and much harder, can follow some of the family connections.
I am enjoying my interaction with my nieces. Please encourage me.

Love, Aunt Susan

Hi Aunt Susan,

We look forward to hearing the rest of the story and about the family reunion. If we don't hear from you before you leave, have a safe and fun trip. We also enjoy hearing from you more too. Xoxoxox
Love, Lexie

Hi Aunt Susan!!
    What a wonderful surprise to wake up to this morning! Your gift is absolutely beautiful (something I would have picked out for myself...we have the same taste!!). I cannot thank you enough for such a sweet gesture and sending home a little piece of Paris to me!!

    Love Always, Jen ❤

Sent from my iPhone

Hi Jen,
    So so glad you liked it. Thanks so much for keeping in touch.
    Love, Aunt Susan

On Jul 30, 2015 Susan Rosler wrote:

Hi girls,
    Please read cousin Tuvia's message below & the story he wrote about his father (this is the same person who sent the story "Mamma").
Much love goes out to you girls. I'm very happy to have people with whom to share family stories.

    Love, Aunt Susan

From: "Tuvia Erez Civil Engineering LTD"
Date: July 30, 2015
To: "Tuvia Erez Civil Engineering LTD"
Subject: Viennese Cremeschnitte
"Dear family and friends,

I, (Tuvia) am attaching an article that I wrote and published about two years ago at the local newspaper about my father, soon after he passed away. I was inspired to translate the article from Hebrew to English after attending a family reunion in Vienna last month. We gathered there from many places: England, Florida, Israel, and Austria. I was amazed to see that while we each lived in a different country (and some of us have never met before), we all shared similar traits. These were the same traits that our parents (all cousins) who grew up in Vienna between the two world wars before escaping Austria in 1938 to different countries, shared. I hope that you will see from the article that our parents perhaps "left Vienna, but Vienna never left them.   Toby (Tuvia)

Viennese Cremeschnitte
By Tuvia (Toby) Erez (Reiss)
This article was originally published in the local newspaper in June 2013, in memory of my father (Tuvia's father), Yitzhak [Kurt] Erez [Reiss], who passed away in May 2013, at age 94.

Photo left: Tuvia's father, Kurt, and sister, Hedi, Vienna, 1926 Photo right: Kurt's photograph on the cover of a book about his life that he published.

We had sat all day home in memory of my father who passed away. As evening began to fall, Shuki (the dog) and I went out to refresh ourselves on the bench in the garden. "My father's story is a long one," I said to Shuki. "It began in nursing home in Naharia (a small town in the north of Israel)." "Interesting," said Bamba (the cat) who sat, without my noticing, on the windowsill. "You always try to act young, but your father's birth-year gives away how old you really are." I ignored the sarcastic comment. "His life story," I said, "on a small scale, is the story of the Jewish people in the twentieth century.

"When my father was 19," I continued, "the Germans annexed Austria. The year was 1938. My father, who was young then, escaped with the youth movement 'Af- Al-Pi' on an illegal immigrant ship headed towards Israel. This was where his wars began: member of the Beitar Company - defending the Jewish settlement, a soldier in the British army fighting the Nazi oppressor, and a soldier in the IDF (Israel Defense Force) in the War of Independence until the Six Day War. Here he met my mother and here he built a family." "All that you can read in a history book, "said Shuki. "Tell us something we don't know. Tell us what kind of a man your father was."

What can I say, my father left Vienna, but Vienna never left him.

My aunt Hedi, my father's sister, told me the following story about their childhood. Every Friday, their mother (my grandmother) made apple strudel (apple cake) - one cake for each member of the family. My father would hide the cake in his closet, lock the closet with a shlissel (key) and every single day he would eat a piece of cake. His sister, on the other hand, would devour her cake in one day. Throughout the rest of the week she would beg and plead for her brother to give her just one more piece of his cake, but he was stubborn and refused. "Control yourself", he would say, "and don't eat all your cake in one day."

"I guess you are like your aunt," said Bamba, "I've seen you devour a pack of peanuts in one go."

The war interrupted his high school studies and his violin lessons. But as an autodidact he knew (almost) everything about music, history, geography, and so forth. When my children would come to me with questions on these topics I would tell them: call your grandpa, he knows the answer. And he never disappointed.

At my other aunt's house on Ben Yehuda Street in Tel Aviv there was a grand piano. At every family gathering he would sit at the piano and ask, "Who has a song request?" To the person making the request he would whisper, "hum me the start of the melody of the song." He would immediately start playing with great feeling and precision as if he had written the melody himself, even if he had never heard it before.

"I remember," said Shuki, "that you too studied violin in your youth." I barely had a chance to answer when Bamba interjected again, "Have you forgotten what they used to say about your violin playing? The neighbors paid you a lot of money not to play."

"His greatest love was the opera." I continued. "Verdi, Mozart and Puccini performed in our house almost every afternoon. He took me to Edis de Philippe's Israeli opera on Allenby Street. For me it was a nightmare. The shrieks, the incomprehensible words, when would it end?! Later in life I decided to give it another chance. My father of course guided me: begin with a light opera like Cavalleria Rusticana by Mascagni and go from there, he said. I did as I was told, and ever since we shared a common love.

"I noticed," said Bamba, "that you have not managed to pass on your love of opera to the rest of the family. Every time you put on opera everyone leaves the room." Ugh, I thought to myself - this cat and his cynicism.

Once, when I was a teenager, I took the bus from my home in central Tel Aviv to the vocational school in Givatayim (a nearby town). Like most teens, I preferred not to see well rather than wear my glasses, which I buried deep in my pocket. By the HaBima Theater I noticed, (in a blur of course), a driver in a private car running rampant, speeding, honking incessantly, trying to pass the bus. The cautious bus driver pulled over to the side to avoid an accident. The car stopped in front of the bus and the driver jumped out, ran to the bus and gestured for him to open the door. When the door opened he came in holding a bag, searched the bus and came directly to me and said, "Toby, you forgot your sandwich bag at home." Two years ago my father moved into a nursing home in a nearby town. There he received a nice modest room and healthy meals suitable for the elderly. "You can go crazy from all the health food," he would say; "bring me something sweet and tasty to eat."

So, once a week I would bring him a Cremeschnitte cake (a vanilla and custard cream cake, popular in Austria). The cake was frozen, straight from the Shoham Bakery fridge in Meona. I would cut the cake into eight pieces with a knife that resembled a saw. Bamba licked his whiskers and grumbled, "You never bring me delicacies like that, only La Cat in the morning, La Cat in the afternoon and La Cat in the evening." "Of course not," I answered, "you would devour the whole cake in one day." "And your father didn't?" asked Shuki.

My father had great self-discipline and an irritating sense of responsibility. Every day in the afternoon he would have his coffee with a piece of cake. At times he would take an additional piece to indulge one of his numerous lady friends at the nursing home.

Two days before he entered the hospital for the last time I brought him the usual Cremeschnitte cake. The following day when I came to visit, he told me it was hard to swallow the cake. Take it for yourself, he said. "But father", I replied, "you know I don't eat cake. We'll leave it here in the fridge. Tomorrow you will feel better and you can have a piece."
"So give it to someone else." He grumbled.
"I don't have anyone to give it to," I said, "let's wait for tomorrow."
"So throw it out." He said.
"Absolutely not!" I said. "Tomorrow you will feel better and have a piece."
He did not reply.

The next day he was moved to the hospital. I came to visit him in the evening. Lying on the bed, pale, eyes closed and mouth covered by an oxygen mask. I gently touched his shoulder. "How do you feel?" I asked softly. He opened his eyes. He removed the oxygen mask with one hand, and held my hand with the other and asked, "Toby, have you thrown out the Cremeschnitte, yet?"

From the corner of my eye I could see Bamba shed a single tear and so did I. That was how he was to the very end: responsibility, order and self-discipline.

Article written by: **Tuvia Erez, Yitzhak's (Kurt) son**

On Jul 30, 2015, Jen Schneider wrote:

How interesting! Love these stories so much!! Thank you for sharing:)
Xoxo
Jen

On Jul 30, 2015, Alexis Schneider wrote:

Hi Aunt Susan,

We love hearing these stories! I shared this with Mikey, my little brother, as he loves learning about all of our distant relatives. He wanted to know if the person writing this story was your first cousin?
Xoxo
Lexie

On Jul 30, 2015 Susan Rosler wrote:

His father, Kurt, the person he's writing about, is my mother's first cousin. I guess Tuvia and I are second cousins. love, Susan

On Aug 9, 2015 Susan Rosler wrote:

Hi Girls,
Listen up. I am planning a driving trip North to New York and beyond during the last week in August. Will you be in town so that I can see you?
Love, Aunt Susan
Hi Aunt Susan,
CAN'T WAIT TO SEE YOU

x0x0x0x0x0x00x0x000x0000x000x000x

On Aug 24, 2015, Jen Schneider wrote:
    You are just too sweeeet!! Can't wait for the visit
Xooxoxxo

On Aug 24, 2015, Susan Rosler wrote:
Hi Girls,
    I'm packing up and expecting to leave tomorrow.
The family photo albums have been a mess for years but yesterday I was
inspired to take pictures of many of the photos and put them into my computer
so that I would have something to show you.   lol
See you soon   Love, Susan

Re: can't wait to see you
Hi Aunt Susan,
I am so excited for the pictures! We are looking forward to your visit.

Mikey, Lexie, Susan, Jen

5 ON THE ROAD AGAIN Keeping in Touch

On Sep 5, 2015, Susan Rosler wrote:

Hi girls,
    Just left New York & on the way to Boston to see my old college buddy,
Gladys. In NY got to see several old friends, Maggie's cousin, Ida & cousins
Royce & Madey.
I have super fond memories of my visit with you.
Regards to your parents & Eve.
    Love, Aunt Susan

Susan and Cousin Madey, father's side, granddaughter of Bernard Mait

Gladys, her neighbor Diane, with Susan

Ida, Maggie's cousin

Hi Girls,

You are ever so lovely. It makes me very happy!!!! So glad we all found each other.

I am presently in Avon Massachusetts, the Boston area, at my friend Gladys 's house. We met on our first trip to Europe, a French study tour, when I was 18. It is through her that I became a French major. Last year, we revisited Paris together.

I am on her porch, after my yoga session, enjoying the breeze and writing to you. Life is wonderful. Regards to all.

Love, Aunt Susan

On Sep 5, 2015, Alexis Schneider wrote:

Hi Aunt Susan,

We are so happy to hear from you! We had such an amazing time with you! I am so grateful that we have reconnected it means so much! Thank you again for the presents I love that they have family history!! Please continue to keep us updated on your trip. XOXO

Much love,
Lexie

6 FAMILY HISTORY: THE NARROW ESCAPE the Decisive Moment

From: Susan Rosler
Subject: LISTEN UP/BIG PROJECT COMING
Date: October 12, 2015
To: Jen Schneider, Alexis Schneider

Hey Girls,
I want to get all the family history stories written down so I plan to be sending you little installments. You may already have heard some of it from me during my visit, but this time it will be written!!! Pay attention and encourage me.
LOVE YOU.
Aunt Susan

Hi Girls,

When Hitler annexed Austria in March, 1938, the Jews were targeted. Many were captured and taken to concentration camps, where they were either killed, or used as workers who died of starvation or disease. One day my father was detained with a group of men. They were forced to lie down and eat dirt while being clubbed. The officer asked if any of them were World War I veterans. My father had an uncle also named Max Rosler who met this requirement. He produced his uncle's veteran ID and was released. Max understood clearly that an escape over the border was his best option. He dyed his hair blond (Aryan style) and visited a man who created and sold false passports for Jews. My mother, your great grandmother, was 21 and faced with the impossible decision of, either taking her 18-month old baby through this, middle-of-the-night RISKY adventure or, leaving her behind with Aunt Fani (my mother's sister). After a heavy-hearted decision, Eve was left with Aunt Fani. My mother and Max boarded the train for Switzerland.
That baby was your grandmother, Eve.
They got off the train at the border and were asked to show their papers. Max, as a blond, handed over the false papers. After the papers were returned, they began to walk. Here is the story told to me by my mother:
"Halten Sie" (stop), said the officer.
Max grabbed my mother and began to run.
She said, "They're calling us, we have to stop."

He said, "No, they'll send us back."

She said, "I can't run so fast." By chance, they ran across a train track and a very long train came by, allowing them to escape into the new night.

She said, "The snow was falling and my hair..." (After all this, she was worried about her hair?!)

My mother and father found their way to the Swiss displaced persons' camp. Mom was safe, but overtaken with worry about her baby. One day, three months later, she returned to her quarters and found Eve sitting on the bed. They held each other for a long time and Eve couldn't let go. Aunt Fani had arranged for the right person to transport her safely to her parents.

Counterclockwise -Fani, Eve, my mother, my grandmother (before saying good-bye to each other)

Susan and her sister, Eve

My parents, Max and Charlotte

Vienna circa 1937: L-R. My mother, father & a friend

7 INVITATIONS FROM UNCLE BERNARD MAIT,
My Father's Connection Gift

My resourceful father held on to the address of his uncle in America and contacted him. Uncle Bernard Mait, signed all the papers and sent the affidavit for the family. Thus they were invited to live in his home in Borough Park, Brooklyn, and I, a few years later, was born in America.

Uncle Bernard Mait, wife, Aunt Ray

On Sep 26, 2015, Alexis Schneider wrote:

Wow! That's incredible. If it wasn't for him who knows if we would even be alive.

Hi Girls,

Uncle Bernard had four children. Thelma's daughter is Madey whom I remembered as a child and young adult, but had not seen for many years. Last year, I had the inspiration to look her up on Facebook and found her to be a remarkably giving person. Last summer I visited her in L.I. during one of my driving trips to New York.

Millie was another of Uncle Bernard's children. This summer (2015) I had the privilege of visiting her daughter, Nancy. She was about five when I last saw her.

Susan, Leslie and her sister, Nancy

The children of Bernard Mait were Thelma, Millie, Elinore, and Monroe. They lived in Franklin Square Long Island. The three sisters were next door to each other and Monroe, across the street.

That's me with peacoat, bobby socks and saddle shoe
(Counter clockwise from L) Wendy, Nancy, Susan (back to camera), Madey,
Leslie

Karen

Hi Aunt Susan,

How adorable!! So funny how things come back in style…I actually have a
black wool type peacoat that I wear all the time!!
Jen

8. VISIT WITH NANCY   "Remind Me Again, How Are We Related?"

The visit with Nancy was quite an impressive adventure. She texted, "remind me again, how are we related?"

After responding to the question, I was invited to dinner where her husband, two daughters, their respective husbands and two grandchildren were in attendance. They lived in a four story house in Massachusetts. The house, much like a museum, was built in 1912 by her husband's grandfather. There were Persian rugs, wood floors, original paintings and woodcarvings done by his grandmother. Authentic mahogany wood furniture, artifacts, stately trimmings with sunlight shining through and, of course, a piano and a ship in a bottle. What splendor!!! I was totally in awe.

We all sat in the living room with hors d'oeuvres. There I was with these historic, impressive people, and I was the guest of honor. They wanted to know all the information on my father's side and when that was thoroughly explained, they were ready for my mother's side. Nancy had a big yellow pad and was taking notes on every detail, names, occupations, etc. Her daughter was note taking on her phone. I asked if they were writing a book. They said no, they wanted the stories and information for their grandchildren and future generations, lest they would be lost.

They were warm and delightful and I was so honored. We then went into the kitchen and sat at the big family table for an amazing meal. Huge shrimp cocktails, corn on the cob, salmon, and home made pie and ice cream. After dinner we retired to the sitting room where they watched my family album slideshow with gusto and gave attention to every detail in each photo. What an evening!!!

9   **BACK TO OCCUPIED VIENNA 1938** and the Dirty Coal Man

My father worshipped his mother and was heartbroken in leaving her behind, but she was in a wheelchair and there was absolutely no way she could run across the border. So Aunt Fani, who was not related to my father's mother, went to see her every day, brought food, and watched over her, until the day she wasn't there. Hitler collected all handicapped people.

Fani put her parents and my grandmother's youngest sister, Tante Pepi, on a ship destined for Palestine. This story, never heard before, was told to me in 1967 during my first visit to Israel and first encounter with Tante Pepi. She spoke only German, which I then studied in college. As a child, since I heard everyone speaking in German, I could understand. However, as no one ever spoke to me, I couldn't speak it.

She explained how the three of them were on a ship that was part of a fleet of five ships. During the journey, there wasn't enough fuel so a coal man came aboard and requested some possessions in payment for coal that he would deliver. Tante Pepi explained how Grossvater, my grandfather, was suspicious and stingy and made only a small donation. The coal man disappeared with some watches, jewelry and other keepsakes. Of course, he never returned.

The passengers then put the men on one side and women on the other. The men threw the beds, tables, chairs and floorboards into the furnace to keep the ship moving. Somehow, the fleet finally made it to Palestine only to discover that the British would not let them dock. The Haganah (Israeli underground) sunk the first of the five ships in a desperate plan to have the survivors, according to international law, taken into the country. However, the passengers didn't survive.

The remaining four ships were sent to a detention camp in Mauritius Island, a dot on the map, off the coast of Madagascar. My grandfather, grandmother and great aunt were among this group. Tante Pepi explained how they spent five years in severe tropical conditions and that my grandmother died of hunger.

I was about 21 and totally mesmerized by Pepi's story. She was charming, delightful and loving. Through her, I was, at last, able to experience the love of my grandmother. After the war, my grandfather and Pepi were taken to Palestine. Pepi was greeted by her two children, Hedi and Kurt. Fani and her husband, Uncle Dory, were reunited with Fani's father, my Grossvater. Pepi stayed with her children.

Fani and Dory brought Grossvater to America to live with my parents in their large apartment in Canarsie, Brooklyn. Everyone's first view of America was *me* on the potty!!!!

Tante Pepi

Hedi and her husband, David

Fani and Grossvater

On Nov 6, 2015, Jen Schneider wrote:

Ah, I was waiting to hear this! That is insane. Goes to show why it's so hard to trust people (coal man). What a crazy story. I look forward to these so much. I hope you don't mind I told my history teacher about you and she was in awe.
Thank you for sharing these treasures.
Xoxo jen

My grandparents

39

10 FANI, THE HEROIC VIENNESE FASHION MODEL

On Nov 6, 2015, Susan Rosler wrote:

Fani was an elegant fashion model for the Krupnick Department store chain in Vienna. Dory, her husband, was the manager. Being the most charming and eligible bachelor in town, all the women were after him but Fani was his favorite. After six years of dating, he finally married her. Six months later, Hitler marched into Austria.

The night before the Anschluss (annexation of Austria into Nazi Germany on March 12, 1938), the Krupnicks (Dory's sister and husband) took heed of the radio announcement and fled to Budapest in a limousine. Dory stayed behind to manage affairs. Hitler had Dory arrested and used him as a propaganda political prisoner. Fani wasn't leaving without her man. She was steadfast in her negotiations with the Nazis. Descriptions of her outfits, including hat, gloves, and handbag, provided colorful newspaper reading material.

While Fani was working on Dory's release, she busily tended to saving the lives of everyone else in the family. Someone was found to deliver Eve to my parents in Switzerland. Fani made regular visits to the visa office and arranged whatever was available on that day. Her sister Rose and family were booked to Trinidad. Thirteen-year- old Hedi had to pass for fourteen and was sent by herself on a youth ship to Palestine.

Fani's brothers Siggy and Nazl had a rendezvous on a particular street. When Nazl arrived, he saw that his
younger brother, Siggy, had been rounded up in a paddy wagon. He started to go toward the wagon, but Siggy motioned to stay back. The vehicle pulled away leaving Nazl standing there in helpless despair. Siggy ended up in Dachau and the incredible Tante Fani, managed to arrange for his release. She begged him to go to Switzerland to be joined with Nazl but he explained how he had to get to Belgium to find his wife and daughter. Hitler marched into Belgium and Siggy, wife, and daughter perished there.

Fani

On Nov 1, 2015, Jen Schneider wrote

Ahh! The suspense is killing me need to hear the rest! I would love to dig thru archives and find a picture of her |Fani| on a poster!
Xxoox jen

Aunt Rose, Marcus
& Son Howard

Harry and his father,
Nazl

11 COUSINS' REUNION IN VIENNA, JUNE 2015

When Tuvia was planning the cousins' reunion, he asked if I could find some more cousins. I emailed Peter, from England, whose lovely wife had died two months before.

"Peter, would you like to go to the cousins' reunion in Vienna?"

He asked, "Are you going?" I hadn't yet decided, but jumped in with a big, "YES" and the arrangements were made. I was so impressed with his courage to venture out at this time.

Peter said, "I'll be staying with my cousin Karl. We're related on my mother's side. I want you to meet him."

Karl was handsome, smiley, and delightful. I wondered how his family managed to stay in Vienna throughout the war and he explained,

"My mother, Suzy, was four at the time and lived with her mother, my grandmother. When the Nazis invaded, they were slated for deportation, but the new Austrian lady of the house, took kindly to them and hid them in the basement for four years.

When Austria was defeated, the Russians came in and occupied the same apartment. The basement people came upstairs and everyone lived together. The Austrian lady asked Suzy's mother to speak for her son, a terrible Nazi, who the Russians were taking away. Suzy's mother said, 'But he was such a big Nazi.'

The Austrian lady answered, 'Yes, I know, he's an asshole, but he's my son.'

In turn, Suzy's mother returned the favor and spoke to the Russians of his heroism and good deeds and he was released."

Karl, laughingly, slapping the walls and doors of the apartment said, "These walls and doors have so many stories to tell of the irony of the Jews, the Austrians and the Russians exchanging places and sharing the space."

Karl's apartment

Suzy and her cousin Peter

L-R: Peter, Susan & Karl

Cousins in Vienna

Counterclockwise Left to Right: Hanna, Jacov, Zvika, Edna, Peter, Susan, David, Liora, Tuvia, Nicole Reiss

12 SEWING FANATIC, Outfits, Outfits, Outfits

On Feb 18, 2016, Jen Schneider wrote:

Hey Aunt Susan…just had a lovely visit with nani |Eve, my sister, her grandmother| when she told me all about your sewing skills. She told me you made beautiful creations that looked professionally made. That is so cool!! Would love to hear more about your talents!!

Xooxox jen

Hi Jen,

For a few years I was a sewing fanatic. I don't have the time for it now because I became fanatic about other   things.

I just spoke to Eve. So sorry this happened but she will heal and all will be well again.

Love to you,
Aunt Susan

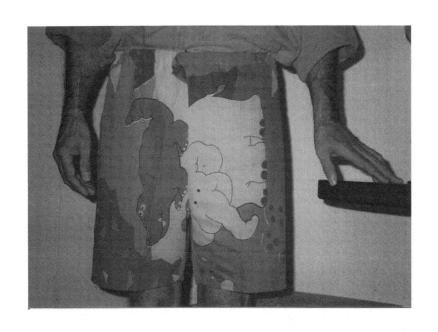

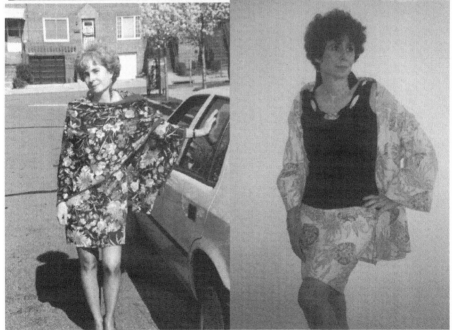

53

56

On Feb 18, 2016, Jen Schneider wrote :

Omg those pictures are amazing. You look like you belong on the cover of vogue. Please tell me the snake around your neck in one is fake!!

Xooxox jen

Hi Girls,

It was real, but not the dangerous kind. He belonged to my friend, Carol, at the Lake House. Love, Susan

13 **MOM AND THE LEOPARD COAT** Many Thousands of Students Awaited.

Mom was always watching out for me. One day when I was in college I received a letter saying that I would not be allowed to become a French teacher because my French speaking skills were not strong enough. Very disheartened, I showed the letter to my mother.

She said, "I'm going up to school to straighten it out."

I explained, "Mom, this isn't like grade school, when you go up to school and speak to the teacher. This is college."

Determined, she reached into the closet and pulled out a leopard remnant, and, in a few minutes, right before my eyes, she fashioned it into a hat. She put on her favorite dress, stockings, high heels, long black leather gloves, new hat, THE LEOPARD coat, and, off we went to school.

We arrived at the office of Dr. Spagnoli, the Italian chairman of the Foreign Language Department. They shook hands and went into the inner office. I remained seated on the bench and waited a while. Eventually, they surfaced. Dr. Spagnoli had a big smile and in his strong Italian accent said,

"Mrs. Rosler, your daughter can have anything she wants. Do you want her to be a teacher?"

My mother in her coat, new hat, and charming Viennese accent hesitated and said, "I don't know what would be good for her, what do you think?"

And thus, my fearless mom and the leopard coat, persuaded him and many thousands of students awaited...

Susan's tenth birthday party/ Counterclockwise- Eve, my mother, friends and me (center)

14 **WINDSOR TING,** My Persistence Paid off

Many years after that, my mother was in the hospital and mentioned that she had a new intern who was so nice. His name was Dr. Ting. The name Windsor Ting flashed through me. About two years later I was leaving my 76 street Manhattan apartment, two blocks from Wagner J.H.S., my first teaching school and cuddled under the arm of my then, tall blond much younger boyfriend, when a gray-haired man with a paunchy stomach called out "Miss Rosler?"

Oh no, how dare a gray-haired man with a pot belly call me Miss Rosler in public, and, still worse, in front of my up-and-coming whatever. I kept turning around looking for this Miss Rosler that he was referring to. Here it comes but even worse than I expected.

"You were my teacher in Wagner Junior High School."

My eyes closed in silent prayer. I've been a high school teacher all my life and that squirt, decked out in his glowing gray hair chooses to have me in junior high school.

"Hi, so what's your name? I can't place you with that *premature* gray hair."

"I'm Mitchell Seleznick."

"Oh yes, first row, third seat, official class, 8 SP 2." (eighth grade, SP-special progress, the top students)

"I've been living on 75th Street for years and I've never seen you," he said.

With all that time to walk around the corner, he chose tonight to blow my cover. My pretended intended, Sandy, smirked while I squirmed. Knowing him, I finally released my breath, his proud gleam meant, "more power to her."

Mitchell said, "Do you remember Windsor Ting?"

I cried out slowly, "Are you still in touch with him?"

"Funny thing, we were just talking about you last night. Windsor never forgot what you did for him and would love to see you again."

"By the way, what are you boys doing these days?"

"Windsor is in a subspecialty surgery program at Columbia Presbyterian Hospital. And I'm at Mt. Sinai, Internal Medicine."

"Hmm," I grunted through my nose.

We arranged a meeting and I took off with my younger man. The worst being over, Sandy was obliged to hear how Windsor became my protege.

8-13 (8 - eighth grade, 13 - high number for low achievement class) was a math class for the slowest kids. We were adding .5 and .3. Only one boy couldn't do any of the work. He looked oriental and arrived in the U.S. two months before. I finally got to the root of the problem. He was depressed, suppressed and regressed.

Since he hadn't studied French or Spanish in his country, the authorities put him on the non-foreign language track, which was the slowest. I thought he would be better off working up to learning French than down to failing all his subjects. The great American way was reprogramming his mind, something like a frontal lobotomy.

"Windsor, I have an idea. Bring in your old math book."

We went to Mr. Hockman, the Assistant Principal.

"Windsor, pick a page." He busily worked out the problems in analytic geometry and calculus.

"Mr. Hockman, do you know the answers?"

He admitted he had no idea.

"That's all right, Windsor does," I replied cheerfully.

After several office visits and much debating with my superior, Mr. H finally conceded to transferring him to 8sp2 where he met Mitchell Seleznick and all the other boys.

Getting back to the present, a week later, Dr. Selznick, Dr. Ting and I had our reunion. After reminiscing about the good old days, I finally got it out. "Windsor, do you remember Mrs. Nussbaum, a patient of yours at Columbia Presbyterian?"

He said, "No." There again was the shy, sad boy of the eighth grade.

"Of course you do. She was hard to forget."

He finally admitted, "I was on the team that did the exploratory and I, along with others that knew and loved her, were horrified at the six month prognosis. It was an untimely end for such a young, vibrant, charming, gracious and giving, sixty-seven year old woman.

She was the one that said thank you when you took a blood sample; the one that never indicated pain, only discomfort; the one that neither cried nor complained wanting to protect her loved ones; the one with the Viennese accent who made us laugh when she said, 'Don't
 buck me' or 'I'll hank in.'"

I nodded and said, "Yes, her last words to me were, 'come home safely.'"

I later wondered why he, at first, denied that he knew her. I guess that, when I asked the question, he too, made the connection. The last name was different, but the face, the same. Her face is what remains for me to cherish and carry on.

Mrs. Nussbaum, (her remarried name), was my mother. And now I know what became of Windsor Ting. *My persistence paid off.*

15 SEWING EVERYWHERE,
Live Your Passion

Healing, after the loss of my mother, took time. A friend said, "Would you like to go to a sewing class with me on Saturdays?"

"Lunch afterwards?" I replied.

"Sure, why not?"

"Great, I'd love to go."

I would have taken a course in auto mechanics, skydiving, anything, for ten weeks to have a friend for lunch and talk. I was excited about my sewing class all week. Finally the day came and we arrived at the 53rd Street YMCA in Manhattan. We sat down in the big high ceilinged room with hard wood mahogany tables. Each table was equipped with a basic black Singer sewing machine. The teacher made the rounds and came to me.

"And what are you going to sew?"

"I have no idea," I replied morosely.

This was repeated for three weeks. Finally, I had an inspiration and purchased colorful, wide-striped fabric and a pajama pattern. The jacket was loose with a raglan sleeve and a long wide band trim around the neck that extended from one side to the other. It had a tie belt around the waist. I learned how to cut the material with the pattern, sew the seams and I was on my way.

This was going to be a birthday gift for my stepfather, Max Nussbaum. He accepted it graciously but I could tell that he really didn't like this style. I later realized that all his pajamas were navy blue. I felt sad but, what the hey! I'll show them all and make it for myself and enjoy wearing it outdoors.

From that time on, I made pant outfits from this same pattern in many different colors, prints, textures, wools, silk, cotton, floral, plaid, polka dot and animal prints. Of course, I revised the pattern here and there. Sometimes it was a jacket and skirt, and, pants could be wide legged, narrow or fitted. The jacket could be longer, shorter, or medium length.

I had lots of fun with the band trim and belt. With help from a sewing neighbor, the puffy sleeve was invented, pinched at the wrist with cuffs and buttons...sometimes, covered buttons.

The sewing machine and fabric had become such close, loyal friends that sometimes, I had to turn away people.

"Sorry Maggie, I can't come over tonight, I'm working on a tailored jacket and trying to figure out how to put in the neck facing." By morning, it was done.

I got a lightweight portable sewing machine and took it everywhere. On the Amtrak, I went to the dining car, put it on a table, plugged it in and away I zoomed.

Long weekends at the Lake House in the New Jersey mountains were enjoyed with blissful hours on the octagon-shaped porch that wrapped around the house. The air was summer-fresh, green, and pinewood scented. From the downhill tree-covered path to the lake, you could hear the laughter of children and splash of the water and, from the distance, they, could chuckle at the hum of my machine. The dock, connected to the lake, was good for cutting out material and Alice was always available for consultations.

"Alice, can we make the puffy sleeve puffier?"

"Sure, let me show you."

Alice was Carol's mother. As a result of my saving Carol's life and finding her a husband, with whom she had three children, Alice granted me unlimited visitation rights to her Lake House. Included with this handsome package, were unlimited questions.

On trips to Europe, I could hand sew. Cruising along the River Thames, I wore one outfit while finishing up another. As for Paris, "it" was impressed with the many colorful outfits and also hat bands to match. On plane rides, the food tray was perfect for cutting out the small pieces for fitted vests.

For every occasion there was an outfit to create. On the way to a wedding, I was finishing up the sequence trim of the left wrist. The mother of the bride said, "Would you believe this dress cost me $800?"

To which I said, "Oh really, it's beautiful. Mine was eight dollars" and I liked mine better.

Sewing on the
airplane

Sewing on
the Amtrak

Sewing on the terrace

Sewing on the beach

Sewing on the Thames River

Sewing in the car

Sewing in the school cafeteria

Sewing on the Lake House
dock

Alice at the Lake House

At the Lake House with Carol's children, Scott, Gregg, and Amy

Paris

16 PHOTOGRAPHY, "What's the Focus?"

At work whenever there was waiting time for a meeting, the sewing machine was ready. At lunch in the cafeteria I had to produce something new for the lunch group every few days.

One day, Larry Sobel, the gentleman of the luncheon table had enough of this ladies' sport. "Susan, do you have any photographs that you've taken?"

I stuttered, "Well a few...?"

"Bring them in," he said.

The next day he critiqued my photos and asked,

"What is the focus here, the tree or the house?"

I didn't know what he was talking about, but followed along. He was a science teacher that obviously took the photography course. The following weekend was a long one so David and I drove to Vermont for the fall foliage and I returned with eight rolls of film, 288 photos.

The whole cafeteria table spent the rest of the year with him asking, "What is the focus?" and never telling me what that meant.

When I started to get it, he asked,

"Why don't you enlarge some of these?"

I wondered, "What for?"

Before you knew it, there were many framed 8x10's, 11x14's and even custom sizes.

Encouraged by a friend, I negotiated an exhibition in a prominent bank on East 86th Street, Manhattan. They displayed the work of local artists in their large corner windows. I placed the framed photos on easels and David helped set it up. But of course, sometimes we argued, so Maggie came to rescue the show. The peaceful, Monet-like natural landscape scenes were on view on this popular street for months. One of my photographs got into Sotheby's and another into two newspapers.

I've been taking photos, and, keeping records of people, events, affairs and parties ever since. To me, now, it seems like I work for Facebook!!!

17 **THE CLOSET,** With a Solid Foundation, You Can Build Anything

One day I looked at the corner of the bedroom and thought that it would be a perfect place to put a closet to store my collections of photo frames and sewing. I didn't know how to build a closet but, with help, I could get it done. I planned on going to the lumberyard on Friday after work, and was beside myself with excitement. Well, there was a big snowstorm that day, but that didn't deter me. In fact, it helped a lot. There were no customers, so the owner had plenty of time and patience to explain how to build a closet. He said, "With a solid foundation and a header, you can build anything." Measurements in hand, he cut the wood and tied the two-by-fours on top of my car. I drove home in the snow and parked at my building.

Saturday morning, strolling down the street, was a young man from Georgia, the former Soviet Union country. He was tall and thin, with brown hair and blue eyes, and was willing to carry up the lumber.

"What are you going to do with all this wood?" He asked.

"I'm going to build a closet. Do you want to help?"

"I don't know how to do that," he replied.

"I'll show you."

So there we were putting the puzzle together. He returned on several subsequent occasions. When he got tired of it, I found someone else, until it was functionally finished.

18 DAVID, THE WEDDING If
He Doesn't Show up, I Want a Refund on the Ring

Time passed and three more closets later, the Maggie and Ida team had introduced David to the scene.

"David, we have been together two years, it's time to get married."

He, at first, said no, as he always does, but then he agreed. We'd meet Wednesday, his day off, at 3:30 when I got home from work. I asked Jerry Wu, the Chinese teacher of English to non-native speakers. "Jerry, can you come with me to do an errand on the way home?"

"Of course," he said.

With Jerry in the passenger seat, I drove around the corner very slowly. Would David be there? I reached the front of my building and, lo and behold, there he was. He opened the door and saw Jerry.

"Who is he? ...Oh, the witness." He said.

I said, "but he doesn't know what he'll be witnessing."

David took the wheel and we drove to the Queens County City Hall.

A clerk said, "The witness needs to sign the registry book."

I asked, "Jerry, do you mind writing your name here?"

Without saying a word, he did it.

"Can you hold my camera and if you see anything to photograph, take a few."

We all stood in a small room with plastic flowers. I wore a white jacket that I made last year and I put together a simple skirt in the same material the night before. I didn't want to start making a whole new outfit, just in case he didn't show up. For the same reason, I didn't tell anyone except for the jeweler. When I bought two used wedding bands from a store, I said, "I'm keeping the receipt and if he doesn't show up, I want my money back, okay?"

The officiator asked for the rings and I presented them.

The justice of the peace pronounced us man and wife. David smiled and I held him tight and gave him a tender, grateful, heartfelt kiss. We signed the book and Jerry knew what to do. We went outside, took some more photos, drove Jerry home and returned to our apartment.

While David prepared dinner, I made some announcement calls.

My friend Diane from work said, "Shit, that's why you were wearing white."

I spoke to my two aunts, Fani and Rose, in Miami Beach. They were both on the extension, but kept saying they didn't understand what I was talking about. I explained it slowly in German. They were in disbelief and shock, as if what I was saying could never happen and was impossible. They finally calmed down and congratulated me.

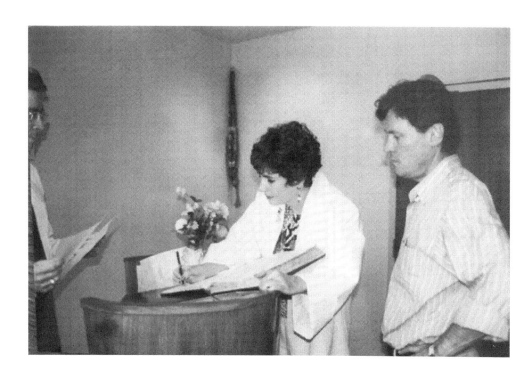

19 DAVID'S CLOSET, If He Can Do It, so Can I

"David, in the corner next to the entrance door, there is a good space for your closet. Will you help me build it?"

"No."

The following day, at work, I asked Jerry. "Jerry, could you help me build a closet?"

"Of course, but I don't know how."

"It will be easy and I have power tools."

"I don't know how to use them."

"I'll show you." So, Jerry and I began to build another closet. Everyday we worked on it. Little by little we made progress. In the evenings, David would come home, prepare dinner, and observed the tiny, busy ants at work. Finally, he thought to himself, "If Jerry can do this, so can I." Bam, Bam, bam, hammer hit nails 1,2,3, and it was done.

left to right: The clerk, Jerry, and David

20 MIAMI BEACH, GLEE GLEE

The following year, I got a year's paid sabbatical leave from teaching and drove to Miami Beach with David and his companion, Letterman, the chocolate Labrador. We rented an apartment in a quaint 1936 art deco building called "The Helen Mar." The corner apartment overflowed with sunlight from eleven large windows. It had ten-foot ceilings, French doors, a fireplace and a tiny balcony that overlooked Lake Pancoast and the ocean.

We would go to moving sales to furnish the apartment. On one such occasion, we were at the house of a gentleman named Socrates. When we finished looking around, we sat and talked. And just to keep busy, I put the man's iguana on my shoulder. Socrates said, "I can tell she really likes you."

"You think so? Why?"

"Look how she closes her eyes when you put your hand on her head."

"Hmm," I said.

I know that David loves all animals and thought he would want her. One thing led to another and we contributed $25 each to become the parents of an iguana named Glee Glee. We put her on the living room floor and watched her walk around. Suddenly, we looked at each other in horror and said, "What are we doing with this creature?"

He said, "I thought you wanted her."

I said, "No, I thought you wanted her."

We realized we were taken and stuck with her. However, to our surprise, we never imagined what an intelligent, lovable, spiritual, cuddly creature she would turn out to be.

She would spend the day on the balcony taking in the sun. In the evening, she would sit inside on her hot rock next to the balcony. She was always watching. If a guest came in, she would be checking them out before they ever noticed she was there. If someone picked her up, she would, of course, close her eyes when they put their hand on her head. I could look at her, move my hand from high to low, and slowly say, "clooose your eyes." Soon she would close her eyes even if I just said it, without hand signals. Then, I would say, "open" in a fast, high-pitched voice and she did it. What communication! She made no sounds, but could say a lot with her eyes.

One day my friend Ken came over with his dog. Ken, David and I went out for a while and gave each dog his own room and Glee Glee, the terrace with the French doors closed. We returned home and Glee Glee was gone. We rushed downstairs to check the garden and returned upstairs in despair.

I hugged David and cried out, "We'll never see her again."

Ken said, "With people relationships, when it's over, it's over. But pets, they come back."

I said, "Maybe, but how would she find her way? She'd have to press the elevator button to the third floor, get off, turn left down the hall and knock on my door. Too complicated."

We went out again, and stepped out of the elevator on the first floor. I took one last look at the tall glass garden doors. Lo and behold, there she was waiting for me still wearing the black leather vest I designed for her.

"Glee Glee," I cried out, swung open the door, scooped her up in my arms and with a tear in my eye gave her the biggest hug ever.

During this fun year, to justify the study sabbatical, I took a black and white photography course. The many funky people in the building served as great subjects for my assignments.

Almost everyday, David and Letterman played at the beach. David threw the ball and Letterman would swim out to retrieve it. This went on, back and forth, for a few hours except for the time Letterman missed seeing the ball and started swimming toward China. With help, and a lot of screaming, we got him back.

I began swimming a little everyday, either in the pool or the ocean, no matter the weather conditions or how icy the waters.

I bought the apartment and a used white baby grand piano.

Saturdays, I joined the Nikki and John team at "The 24 Carat" clothing store on Lincoln Road. Nikki played the piano,

John sang and I danced. I was allowed to share the compliments but not the tips. Still, there was time for some sewing and piano lessons with Nikki. The grand ole piano came alive, danced and hopped to the music of Nikki's classic show tunes.

David, Letterman & Glee Glee

Photo by Dale Stine

21 **REGO PARK, QUEENS,** Arm in Arm, the Labrador and the Iguana

The drive up north: David at the wheel, the passenger with some hand sewing, the dog in the back seat and the iguana on the shelf. Back to Rego Park, Queens, for two years until retirement.

When I put on the dance music, Letterman, who jumped and barked, was a distraction, but Glee Glee bobbed her head and lifted her hands, left then right, gracefully to the music.

I'd put her out on the terrace to do her business. When she was done, she'd tap on the screen door. And when I said, "I'm coming," she'd stop tapping and wait.

On a warm day in December, she enjoyed sunning herself on the terrace chaise lounge. On this day, as she watched me from the bedroom window, she said to herself,

"She's in the mirror with the hair and the make up, getting ready to go out. I know she's going to forget that I'm out here. It's already starting to get cold. I have to get her attention. I need a plan. I'll keep watching until she turns her head this way, and in that split second, I'll jump off the chaise lounge. The chair will move, make some noise and that will remind her to bring me inside."

Fortunately for my clever, cold-blooded creature, her plan worked.

It was such a pleasure to see this odd couple, the Labrador and the iguana, standing at the door together, arm in arm, waiting for me to come home from work.

One time David and I were packing for the weekend, gathering stuff and putting in this and that. Glee Glee watched from her cardboard box. Suddenly we carried all suitcases and things with Letterman and proceeded to the door. Glee Glee said to herself, "What, they're leaving without me. No way!"

She jumped out of her box ran toward the door, sauntered up the two steps of the sunken living room, looked up and said, "You're NOT leaving without me?"

I said, "David, we have to take her."
He nodded. I picked her up in my arms and off to the Lake House in the mountains we went.

Arm in Arm, the Labrador and the Iguana

22 LAST TWO YEARS OF TEACHING, Always Inventing Systems

The last two years of teaching were the best. The chairman was fabulous, supportive and funny. The teachers in the department were numerous, unified and party loving. They put on an International Festival where teachers and students performed together on the stage to "Men in Black," sunglasses and all. My peers treated me with honor and relished in my escapades. Dance parties with them were always fun. Since I never could follow anyone's steps, I had to dance alone, with a pole, or a broom, or whatever was available.

I loved classroom teaching. Since I didn't allow any talking, even whispering, in the classroom, you could hear a pin drop and only the squeak of my boots as I walked down the aisles checking the homework and correcting their writing.

I had invented many systems and routines during the time to prevent talking and to keep them working. The class monitor would write the prepared four sentences from my plan book on the left corner chalkboard in English. While everyone worked on the translation in their notebook, four students would write their translation into Spanish on the right corner board. We would correct them together and read them in unison. While I was taking attendance and walking from student to student, checking homework, they would memorize the Spanish sentences by looking at English cues.

Now the game that I invented would start. I'd pick a number from 1 to 4 and call on someone to recite. He would look at the English sentence on the left, no peeking or turning his head and recite the sentence in Spanish. If he made no mistakes, he would get a credit (check mark on his seating plan card). They worked liked crazy for these credits, which were the major part of their grade. How many credits was a 90? a big bunch, 80 was a smaller bunch, and so on. The sentences were designed to be a sequential growth of the vocabulary and grammar. Following this, new vocabulary and new material was presented.

Each day's "perfectly designed" four sentences were created during the planning period in the ladies' teachers' room. I needed to get all the preparation done during this period in order not to take any of it home. So in this shared space, no talking was allowed. The teachers would enter the restroom tiptoeing and bent over with one finger on their lips indicating "sh." They imitated me with a smile and all my planning was accomplished during this time.

I returned back to class from the teachers' room, in a long circle skirt, a tailored suit, a two piece pajama outfit with or without puffy sleeves, or, pants and a fitted vest, all with matching scarves: each day a different one, from the rotational system. I walked proudly & cheerfully with a pencil behind my ear and a student carrying my small 5x7 notebook.

I noticed I had no trouble walking, but carrying things and standing in one place gave me muscle knots. The doctor called it fibromyalgia and I, again, invented systems around it.

Students and teachers
performing "Men in Black"

23 BACK TO MIAMI BEACH, RETIREMENT, 1999, "Everyone Has Something"

The caravan to Miami Beach for the permanent move included David, wearing a baseball cap on backwards, driving the 14-foot truck filled to the brim with boxes, Letterman in the passenger seat with a serious professional look, a tall palm tree between them, Glee Glee on the back shelf, and David's red Mitsubishi car trailing behind on a hook. I followed, baggage-free, in my shiny new red Honda.

Among my many possessions was an article on fibromyalgia. After finally learning how to pronounce it, I kept repeating it. I presented it to Vidar, the office manager.

"Vidar," I said cheerfully, "Here is an article that will explain everything about me."

Vidar, with his wry sense of humor said, "Fine, I'll file it under your name."

Juan, a very tall, annoying occupant of the building was always up and down with his greyhound and constantly picking on me.

One day he looked down at me and said in a slow sinister voice, "Everyone has something," referring to my fibromyalgia.

Although he was quite a nasty guy, that statement taught me a lot.

The fibromyalgia article explained that you would be depressed and anxious. The best thing to do was exercise, but you won't want to do it. Being the rebel that I am, I had to defy this. I swam in the ocean or pool every winter day, including the coldest ones. It was really hard to get into the icy water, but once I jumped in and swam across and back, I no longer noticed the chill. I felt like Tarzan after performing a great task. I was invincible and could do something that no one else would do.

The garden was filled with exotic trees, greens, bamboo and palms, an ocean view, and breezes. Everywhere were the sights and sounds of pelicans, sea gulls, egrets, and hummingbirds. From my balcony and all the windows I could see stingrays, manatees, and every possible boat including sculling teams.

I was on the board of directors at the Helen Mar but got into trouble when I insisted that the management company was corrupt, dishonest and messing in the finances. Some agreed but didn't want to deal with it. In order not to hear about it anymore, to my surprise, they got rid of me instead of it. My beautiful tropical paradise had turned into enemy territory.

24 SUZANNE, I Was Careful not to Get into the Story

Just in time to save me, out of the blue, I got a call from Maggie's sister, Dina, who lived in New Mexico. She wanted to know if I was going to New York today, by chance.

"No, but I'm writing a letter to the condo board. Maybe you can help."

"Well, I'm packing and leaving today so why don't you call Suzanne, my friend that lives in Fort Lauderdale? She was in a condo once and is very helpful."

"Hello Suzanne, Dina suggested I call you. Maybe we can meet some time."

"Sure, When?"

"Today?"

"Today?? Yes, of course."

Directions, in hand, I was on my way to Suzanne's. I had alienated everyone in my area with my politics and felt it all around. I couldn't wait to get out of town. It was an hour's drive to her house. When I reached my destination, I found an incredible oasis. The street was quiet and sunny with many green trees and the birds were singing announcing my arrival. The front garden had roses, lilies, lilacs, daisies, chrysanthemums and other things I didn't know about.

Inside the house was soft zen music, fresh aromas with sunlight, mirrors and windows reflecting the happy life of birds, flowers, trees, butterflies, frogs, critters and turtles. Her decor was colorful and filled with her paintings and her framed photographs of exotic travel scenes. The second bedroom was wallpapered in leopard with stuffed animals representing a peaceful jungle. The living room had a spacious, high, cathedral ceiling and everything was decorated in a natural tasteful decor. **All** created and maintained by her.

Even the small back garden that could be seen from the sliding-door picture window, was her creation with roses and every possible herb. In the center was a small shrine where she buried the urns of her parents. She said, "They got along better than ever since they had been there."

Suzanne had a modest pension and an excellent sense of humor. She made a joke of everything. It was such a pleasure visiting her that it became a regular thing for Fridays.

In addition, she was available every time I needed an emergency escape from someone or something. She used to frequent Siddha yoga in South Fallsburg, N.Y. and meditated regularly.

When I arrived, we'd sit in the peace for a while and then go out to lunch and shopping. She always said that she was happy not to have to make the trip to my place and therefore, she felt it was fair if we only shopped for my things. What heaven!!!! Everything I needed was taken care of with Suzanne; the orange bathroom towels, the dehumidifier, the bargains at my favorite clothing store. I could bring over my latest fabric selections and she would help me create my fashions. I brought my laptop and she, with that great artistic eye, would help select the best photos.

Alas, one day I called with a request to visit and she said that it was not a good idea. After months of subsequent calls, she said the same thing. I wondered what I had done to lose my good friend, Suzanne. Would I dare to take the hour drive and stop over unannounced?

One day, I walked up to the house, rang the bell and a tall woman opened the door and let me in.

I saw Suzanne sitting in a rocking chair in the living room. She was much thinner and had bright red hair. I sat down and she explained that she was diagnosed with a progressive, degenerative disease called supra nuclear palsy. She didn't want me or anyone else to visit because she felt that she had nothing to offer. We talked for a few hours and I returned home after dark. This information was horrible but, on the good side, I reunited with my dear friend and could visit under the new circumstances.

I was very careful not to get into the story. I looked up the illness on the Internet and stuck to the facts. I did not picture anything nor think about it. I would simply continue to visit and enjoy her amazing presence. The next time I came, she was in bed in her exquisitely decorated bedroom. I gave her a hug and she was quivering to cry but I stopped her and said that it wasn't ALL bad.

"Look at the beautiful curtains. Other people get sick and are in far worse circumstances."

From her bed, Suzanne entertained. She always greeted me with a smile and a chuckle. We chatted for hours. When I lamented about the condo, choir issues and the difficulties of choosing a new dentist, she delivered her funniest line. In her unique, and comical style she said,

"I don't know WHAT I would do if I had your problems."

I brought over a VCR and a pile of comedies. We watched, laughed, and enjoyed each other's company. One sunny afternoon, I rushed over with the "Sound of Music" video. It was a very special day because her caregiver had moved her to the extra bed in the big dining room. The large room with many windows was filled with light and we were surrounded, embraced and enfolded in total peace, love and divine energy.

Alas, she explained, because of the "disease" as she jokingly called it, she couldn't really see the TV anymore. So I brought a CD player and some discs of sermons, songs and meditations. Since she was an avid reader, I downloaded several audio books. Together, we experienced the latest best sellers. She gracefully mastered the position of the buttons on the CD player and could continue on her own.

One afternoon, as soon as she heard me entering the room, she joyfully and exuberantly announced, "I'm in love!"

"Pray tell, with whom?" I asked.

"Rev. Chris Jackson" (The reverend on the CD's.)

As time moved ahead, her speech slurred more and more and it was becoming difficult to understand what she was saying. I knew that I needed to plan some stories to tell before I arrived. I would ask yes and no questions. She learned from someone to hold up two fingers for "yes" and one finger for "no."

David began driving me and I would visit in the evening. She would be lying in her bed in total darkness because the light bothered her eyes. Each time I came, she was neither crying nor depressed. She was peacefully resting. She lit up when she heard me and held up three fingers, jokingly. I knew that meant three hours of sleep at night. It was, as everything else, part of the "disease"!

One of the stories I told her was about Facebook and how I reconnected with childhood friends from the block.

"Do you have any old friends that you'd like me to look up?"

She indicated yes. But how was I going to get the name, I wondered? I thought of the alphabet game that I must have seen in a movie.

"I'm going to start the alphabet and show me a 'yes' when I reach the letter of the last name."

I copied down what came out A B O U F.

"Abouf" I said, "are you sure? What kind of name is that? No, it can't be Abouf, there's no such name."

She indicated, "yes" and roared with laughter.

"No, not ABOUF it can't be".

She kept rolling and roaring so much that Myrtle, her caretaker, came in to find out what was going on and we all laughed.

"Abouf, noooo, are you sure?"

Without being able to speak, Suzanne managed to tell a joke that made everyone laugh. I knew she was putting me on but we all had fun.

Her two sisters, son, daughter, three grandchildren, Myrtle and other family friends attended the Memorial Service. There were photos of her smiling and many stories told. After they finished, I finally dared to ask to tell mine: Abouf and all the other funny things she said and did. They all laughed remembering her generous spirit and amazing soul. Her essence filled the air and we were all, *forever*, enriched by her presence.

The Memorial Service was April, 2014.
(This photo of Suzanne that popped out among my possessions)

On May 1, 2017, at 2:00 PM, Susan Rosler wrote to Suzanne's daughter, Heather:

Hi Heather,

Thinking of your mom all the time. She is that happy amazing spirit that guides us in everything that we do.

Do you have a smiling photo of her to send me?

From: Heather Geraci
Subject: Re: Suzanne
Date: May 1, 2017 at 8:39:50 PM EDT
To: Susan Rosler

Hi Susan!
So great to hear from you...and so interesting. I always think about my mom but for some reason I have been really thinking about her a lot in the last few days. My cousin sent me this picture yesterday out of the blue. Makes me think my mom is all around us.

I always think about what a special friend you were to her. You supported her so much and I will never forget that.
Hope you and the family are doing well. So happy you reached out.

Lots of love, Heather

25 CHOIR, Never Give Up

Back-tracking with the choir, when I first saw them at Unity on the Bay, spiritual community, it was the year 2000. They were jumping and dancing. What fun!

I asked one of the choir people, "Can I join?"

He said, "Of course."

"But I can't sing."

"That's Ok."

"I can't even carry a tune."

"No problem."

I joined, keeping my out-of-pitch voice, low-key and quiet. I was an enthusiastic weekly participant. Whenever they wanted to sing for some benefit, I was always available. On Sunday services, my style of jumping and dancing to the music delivered their message of joy, love, acceptance of all, letting go, and oneness.

I heard many testimonials: One man, who later became an administrator said, "The first time I came to UOTB and saw you up there doing your thing and having so much fun, I knew that this was the place for me."

But alas, the day came, when the choir director called me aside and told me that there was a policy change and that I needed to improve my singing skills to sing with the group on Sundays, and I could return in the future. I knew that it would take a LONG time for my return as a singer. It took NINE years and several director changes!!

Since I had found my center and did not want to leave, I opted to just practice at rehearsals but not perform at Sunday services. Soon, the director said, "I need a non-singing assistant. Would you like to do that?"

I eagerly said yes and became a very busy beaver. I bought a Mac, trained at the Apple store and filed all the mp3's, pdf's, photos, and word documents. I took photos of every party, concert, birthday, event, Sunday group photos, individual ID photos, etc. and communicated all information via email or text. I kept data records of members, sent out prayers, and posted birthdays with a photo, and, each person had his own birthday poem. I also recruited the new members and taught them how to read music.

In my spare time, I worked on my singing: I got an iPad on which I had a keyboard app and spent afternoons playing the weekly songs and matching pitch. I took the iPad everywhere: Amtrak, plane, the car, the dentist office and

Europe. I joined the Spanish choir and took private lessons with everyone, starting with how to breathe, and yes, NINE years later I could sing with the group as an equal. I never gave up. Tenacity was my middle name.

Dale Stine, the current director, said of me, "She's the choir mom, the glue that holds everything together. She copied and filed recordings of every song the choir has ever done. Ask her for a song, and before you know it, it's there!"

<Two photos by Pamela Scheel

Photo by Maurizio Martinoli

Dale Stine, Director of the Unity on the Bay Choir

photo by Mamo

122

Chaplains of Unity on the Bay

26 YOGA, Prescription for Well-Being

One day I realized that each wrist hurt when flexed so I wore a brace till they healed. Then my thumb became a trigger thumb and shifted off its socket. I noticed other fingers began to hurt in the same way. The orthopedist gave me a cortisone injection, which turned out to be a temporary solution. An operation on my thumb worked. After the wound healed the physical therapy diagrams made me understand that exercising the fingers for me was necessary. These fingers pointed me to yoga.

In the past, I had taken a class here and there. I got the Eric Schiffman, Ali McGraw, *Mind Body and Spirit* DVD which is now available on line. I put on the DVD and from the couch observed David doing the poses. This scenario went on for a while, David on the yoga mat and me watching from the couch. I got up to try something but returned back to my comfort zone.

Eventually, I actually got up long enough to get through the tape and noticed how much better I felt. David and I fell into an inexpensive yoga class. I followed the teacher to her regular yoga studio. I was there once a week, twice a week, then three times and suddenly I was a member that practiced six mornings a week.

No more wrist or finger issues and the fibromyalgia was mainly out of the way. Downward dog, head stands, hand stands, yoga retreats, teacher training and soon I wouldn't travel without my yoga DVD, laptop and mat. A friend had onset of Parkinson's and, sure enough, I googled yoga for Parkinson's and there it was. Another friend mentioned stenosis, and again, there it was, on Google. I bet yoga addresses most conditions. The DVD's message of oneness of mind, body and spirit trains you to focus on the breath in order to keep the mind still and at peace. The exercise of every muscle in the body keeps the pain out and is the strength and foundation of my life. I couldn't manage without it.

Tropical Vinyasa with Paul Toliuszsis andAmy Danheim, founders

Yoga retreat with Ewa Josefsson, Costa Rica   photos by Jonathan Hökklo

Teacher Training, Paul Toliuszis

Yoga class with Jason Lawner

Class with Paula Walker

Study parties during Teacher Training

Carlos Tao, one of my teachers

Amy Litt Rabin at Tropical Vinyassa

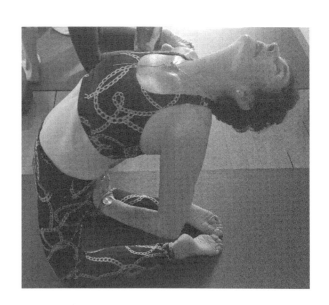

Photos & instruction by Ewa Josefsson

The following series: photos and instruction by **Beth Ogden**

141

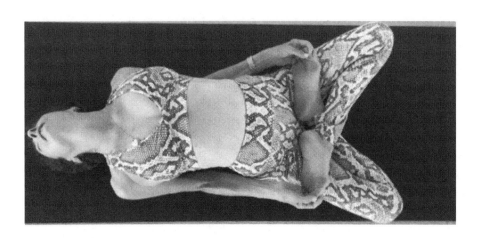

Cobra yoga ensemble, courtesy of *Glimpse Miami*

27 YOGA TRIUMPHS, Many roads lead to yoga

At the heart of the yoga community is Deneen who has *Lyme* disease. She practices several days a week and can do almost any pose with incredible skill and grace.

Still with some pain, she breathes, flexes through it and is never seen without a smile or a hello. After class she offers personal weight training sessions to some of the more advanced yoginis.

Wendy has fibromyalgia and had considered herself very sick for a number of years. During that time, she mainly rested in bed, in pain and unable to accomplish much. She found yoga and we all marvel at her progress. She makes us laugh as she jokes through a class with her forward bends, downward dogs, vinyasas and pigeon poses always asking when is the sivasana (final resting pose). Her stamina, mood and agility are steadily increasing.

Claudia had sciatica pains but with regular practice, her issues are gone.

Bru had a major back ailment that brought her to yoga hoping to avoid surgery. She decided on the surgery, and is now rehabilitating perfectly during her yoga classes.

When Peter had severe low back pain, he took an MRI and was considering surgery. In the interim, he tried yoga and had some private lessons with Amy Litt Rabin who corrected his stance, form, and alignment. He now walks tall and is pain free.

Doncha had a car accident in which the car rolled over and she barely made it to the hospital alive. She has returned triumphantly to her yoga classes, smiling all the way through her rehabilitation.

Among the 14 lucky people in our teacher training group was Valeria. Very active in gymnastics and running, she suffered an injury that destroyed her hamstring. After receiving a donor hamstring and surgery, she arrived at yoga. Her down dogs are accomplished with the aid of blocks and with a genuine bright smile, she adjusts to her new life style.

Jack had a hip replacement and always makes us laugh when he performs his difficult one-armed handstand, upside down, mouth moving and still telling jokes.

28 MARINA YASHINA, THE RUSSIAN RESTORATION PAINTER, Don't Ever Take Anyone or Anything for Granted

While sitting at the Mexican restaurant with Hanny after yoga class enjoying our usual cappuccino with chips, red salsa and an occasional guacamole, I began telling her of my recent phone conversation with Marina, my Russian friend.

Hanny was traveling a lot: deep sea diving, skiing, hiking, exploring, even a yoga retreat in South Africa. But when she was in town, we could spend hours talking about whatever came up. She was a great listener and wanted to know about anything that came out of my head. Hanging out with her was among my most satisfying and relaxing pleasures.

Our favorite table was under a tree, giving us shade and allowing us to watch the sunlight and feel the light breeze. The table was covered with a red, blue, green, orange and grey fringed, horizontally striped Mexican blanket and a terra cotta clay pot containing a red flower. Under the table were two long wooden benches with cane seats and comfy red cushions trimmed with pompoms.

Hanny said, "Who is your friend Marina?"

I told her, "A long time ago, I saw the movie *Dr. Zhivago*." The rest of the story went like this:

I was so taken with the romanticism of czarist Russia that I vowed that I would visit Moscow by summer, and before then, learn some basic Russian. I got *The Living Language Series*, played the records, and the Russian man on the recording kept me company every day until I was ready to go in July.

While exploring the interior of St. Basil's Cathedral, the exquisite show piece of the czars, a young woman, who was on a scaffold painting the frescoes, called down to me,

"*Vwi evretsky*? [Are you Jewish?]"

"*Da Konyeshna* [Yes, of course.]"

She came down from the scaffold and we sat in a comfortable corner where we spoke. She became my guide and took me everywhere. She figured out my vocabulary and understood how to build on it. Marina Yashina was a restoration painter for the Kremlin, the Pushkin Museum and St. Basil's. Awestruck by her importance, working on the top paintings of the world, she was the Soviet Union's finest.

I returned home and she wrote letters, sent drawings and her photographs of St. Basil's Cathedral.

147

Five years later I got a call from the United Hias organization about my relatives in the Soviet Union.

"Yes, of course, you mean my cousin."

"How are you related?"

"Well it's so complicated that if she told you the story and I explained it, it could be very different, but we are cousins."

"She and her daughter are out of the Soviet Union and if you would sponsor them, they could come to New York."

"Her daughter? How old is this daughter?"

"Seven."

"Oh, yes, I remember, there was a baby. We-e-e-ll, ok. What do I have to do?"

"Come to the office and sign papers."

The exciting day came and a friend and I picked them up. I took little Olga to school and brought Marina to the Metropolitan Museum to ask about a job. They referred me to an alphabetical list of restorers. The first one was Gustav Berger. I called, and voilà, a job. Pay was not great but she received a superior training. Berger invented BEVA 371 which was a special glue used by most restorers. She made the front page of the NY Times when Picasso's *Guernica* came to the U.S. after Franco's death in 1975. Of course, her name didn't appear in the article. The restoration was credited to Gustav Berger, but we know she did the work.

One day I asked Marina why he always walked around with the same paper shopping bag.

Marina said, "I think he's carrying a million dollars in that bag!!!"

During the evenings Marina, speaking in Russian, invented words with charades and sign language to perform Solzhenitsyn stories of the Gulag and others.

Her mother was once on a train with her older brother when he was an infant and was asked to show papers. She had papers for herself but none for the baby. So they were put off the train. Mother and baby sat alone on a bench in an isolated station, snow everywhere, temperatures way below freezing and no food in sight. The baby died.

On a lighter note, she told many stories of the Rabbi and the chicken. After more stories and excellent Russian language training from a grateful guest, I signed a few more stacks of papers for additional *cousins*.

I had eight months of entertainment and training when Marina and little Olga found an apartment nearby with one of the *cousins*. I was always the guest of honor, the cousin from America, for pyrogy, blintzes, borscht with sour cream and do you want some *nervni chai?*-- the name she made up for chamomile tea. Thus, the training continued and we always spoke in Russian.

Cousin Irina, years later said, "When Susanna walked out in her mink coat, she would stop traffic."

For them, I was a superstar. Time went by and Marina and I remained friends. Eventually, she bought a house with *cousin* Svetlana in Mastic Beach, near Fire Island.

The rustic wooden house and garden, much of it built and designed by Marina, was primitive and charming.

Letterman especially, enjoyed his visits running around like crazy inside the fenced-in garden.

Marina developed her own impressionistic-like painting style that I cherished. She had given me some paintings and others I bought. Later, she moved to Cold Spring Harbor, New York, on the Hudson River where she opened the Marina Gallery.

During her visit to Miami Beach, she took some snapshots of me. One day she called and said that she made a very large painting of me from a photograph and sent me a picture of it, and, did I want the painting? I stuttered and stammered and couldn't decide if I really liked it or if I had room for it. By the way, I always have a problem making decisions. I showed the photographed copy of it to everyone that would listen to me.

Jeff, a neighbor, said, "This is an IMPORTANT painting."

"Really? Why is it important?"

"Because it is from the back.'"

"Ohhhhh?"

Still debating, I finally called Marina and, with conviction, said, "I want the painting."

Marina said, "It was hanging in the gallery and I sold it."

"What! Get it back. I'll buy it for more."

"I'll never find the man."

"Look in the records."

She snorted with a laugh, "what records?"

"Don't worry," she said. "I'll make you another one but not exactly the same."

"No, I want the same one!!" I persisted.

"But I'm an artist I can't make the same one. I have to change something. I'll make it from the front."

"No, no, no, it has to be from the back."

"Let me think about it."

The time went by and I didn't hear from her. I didn't rush to call because maybe I wouldn't like the changed version.

Finally I called. "Hi Marina."

"I'm sick," she said.

"What do you mean?"

"I have a brain tumor." My heart fell out of me. *Marina…* I said to myself. All I could think of repeatedly: *"Don't ever take anyone or anything for granted."*

Back to the present:

"So Hanny, how will I get my painting?"

We laughed at the absurdity of the importance of a painting that I didn't, at first, want. And, were we more concerned about the painting than Marina? I could hear Maggie's voice in the background.

"Someone will come who can paint the original, and who knows, maybe it doesn't have to be an exact copy?"

Hanny and Susan at the Mexican restaurant

photos by Marina Yashina

The Painting by Marina Yashina (from the back)

29 FRENCH, So much Is Possible When You Change a Pattern

When I was 18, I decided to go to Europe. Trying to find a friend to travel with was a hassle, so I looked for tours. There was bicycling or hosteling, too difficult. Ah, a French study tour. I scored 98's consistently in high school French. That would be easy. However, I discovered that sitting on tour buses puzzling out the guide's French stories was a major headache. Tolerating insults from sophisticated French majors was also not pleasant. "Don't speak, it's grating on my ears," they taunted.

But on this tour, I met Gladys from my hometown, Brooklyn, and we became life-long friends. She was a French major and a great role model so that's how it all started.

The beginning courses in college French were difficult for me. Although I had all those 98's in H.S., I couldn't speak or comprehend a word. When the ForeignLanguage Chairman, my mother, the leopard coat and hat met, we agreed that I had to improve my skills. For my next summer in Paris, I would eat, think and dream only in French.

On this economy mission, I found a room in the suburbs for forty cents a night. My room, upstairs by the roof, had a bathroom with a stove for hot water and coffee. I had instant coffee for breakfast with last night's bread. Since my watch was not reliable, I stood on the roof, and barked out, "Pardon, quelle heure est-il? Then off to Paris by metro! My usual stop was the Latin Quarter's, Boulevard St Michel. My poor sense of direction served me well. I'd ask how to find a place and before I knew it, the person would accompany me. Next destination, next person, maybe stop for coffee, maybe a long walk. It didn't matter with whom I spoke, as long as it was in French.

There were four summers in Paris and for the winter, French roommates. One roommate wanted the window open for fresh air in zero degrees. She'd open, I'd close and she'd open again. The discussions were all in French. It is amazing how much you can learn from an impertinent person.

When I got to speak again with the Foreign Language Chairman, who was Italian, I evaluated him. He had a greater and more erudite vocabulary but my accent was FAR superior to his. My mission was accomplished!

I enrolled in graduate school at Brooklyn College and took 30 graduate credits toward a Master's Degree in French Literature. I didn't take the final step of the comprehensive exam and thesis course because I heard that they failed a few people at that level and it wasn't required for my teaching job or anything else.

But as things changed, I had to learn Spanish in a hurry, take courses, get a license, go to Barcelona, study on the beach of Palma de Mallorca, Spanish roommates, etc. New requirements came up and I needed a Master's Degree. It could be in French literature, or, French Education. My options were to get the degree in education by taking one education course that could be done in a weekend, or, get the straight master's in French literature by taking that old scary comprehensive exam and thesis course.

Well you know me, I had to journey through the purer and more difficult path. But to secure the deadline, I reluctantly took the education course first. It would last only a weekend, and I became very angry at the absurdity and hypocrisy of course simplifications.

I handed in my official transcript, as requested, and then got a phone call at my home saying, "You have to bring in your college degree."

"But why do I need that, you have the transcripts."

"Don't make it a big deal, just bring it in."

I got off the phone, and angrily stared at my floor-to-ceiling bookcase that was very securely fastened to the brick wall and had been there for around fifteen years. Shockingly, the bookcase popped off the wall and all the books slid down. OMG I am powerful!!! If only I could use that for good.

I got through the comprehensive exam in French literature and was ready for the thesis course. The leftover topic was the aesthetics of Chateaubriand as seen in his two books, *René* and *Atala*.

My pattern in writing college papers was always the same. I would research and gather every aspect of the topic, including in-depth, inventive related ones, only to discover that I was very close to the deadline and had to leave out most of it. In the end, I frantically put something together with guaranteed mediocre results… and the typing!!!

Margot, who I had matched up with her current husband, reciprocated. She stepped in saying, "I know all about this stuff." Coming directly from the library, she said, "Here is a book on this topic. Be sure to include the death scene and all its colors. I'll be back to check on you in a few days." And this is how she organized and paced me.

Since I was working full time, most of the work on the thesis paper was only started during the winter break.

Day and night, I sat with the books and material and wrote in French. I was in the romantic "mal du cycle" and channeled Chateaubriand himself. I carefully chose my words and was guided by a thesaurus and Margot's advice.

Finally done and typed, only the accent marks were missing. I dashed them in on the drive from Manhattan to Brooklyn, and, racing up the three flights of stairs. Huffing and puffing, I presented my thesis to Professor Molnar.

"Here is the paper," I said, "but some accent marks are still missing."

He responded dryly, "It's all right, I know where they are."

Remembering me from the past, he didn't expect much. A week later, he returned all the thesis papers. He handed me mine, and announced, "This was the biggest surprise of all. It was the only 'A' paper and even aesthetically beautiful."

I cried and never forgot that moment. *So much is possible when you change a pattern.*

30   TEOFIL'S DIARY IN ENGLISH

On September 6, 2016, Tuvia sent out an email saying that Teofil's diary had been translated into English and could be purchased on Amazon.com.

Oh wowwwww, finally. I bought one for myself and then sent one to each of my nephew's children, Jen, Lexie and Mikey. Then, of course, I had to send one to Melissa, my great niece, Amy's daughter. But, of course, I had to get a copy for Hanny (yoga) and Helen (choir). Then there were birthdays in the choir and I couldn't think of what to get and there it was, the perfect gift.

Then, of course, Jude and Ellen Frazier, cousin Peter in England, Ewa Joseffson- the yoga teacher that named my dog, Teri DeSario- my voice teacher that convinced me to get a dog and write a book...and so on...oops another obsession.

From: *"Tuvia Erez Civil Engineering LTD"*
"In the Line of Fire"
Date: September 6, 2016
To: "Tuvia Erez Civil Engineering LTD"

Dear Friends & Family,

New book: "In the Line of Fire"
Tuvia wrote:

During the First World War that took place 100 years ago from 1914-1918, a soldier in the Austro-Hungarian army, Teofil Tobias Reiss, fought in the trenches on the Russian front and later on the Italian front. Teofil, a professional soldier, a lady's man, and a proud Jew – my grandfather, recorded his daily experiences in a journal he carried with him throughout the conflict. This journal has been passed down for three generations, and has now been translated into English and made into a book, titled "In the Line of Fire."

According to 'Haarerz,' a leading Israeli newspaper, the book is "a fascinating human record, a rare testimony of a brave soldier, and a convincing image of a decent man in a pointless war." Reiss's candor and

"innocence which inspires trustworthiness" as Haaretz notes, will keep readers turning pages, as Teofil's touching personal account of wartime horrors, bravery, and romance unfolds.

The book has been published by Amazon under the title: *In the Line of Fire*: A Soldier's Diary WW1 1914-1918 by Teofil Tobias Reiss

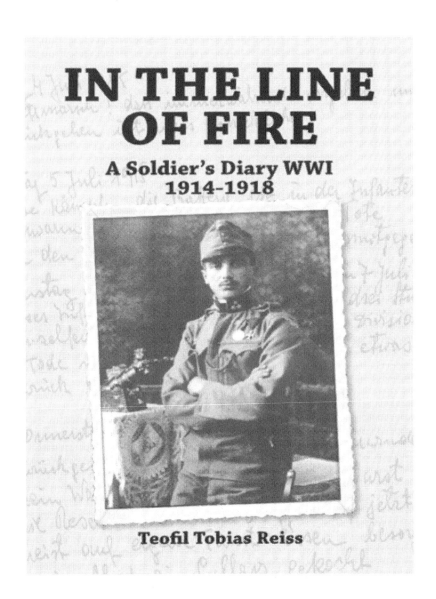

31   RAMA, Makes You Laugh

Years after Letterman was gone, I began interviewing all the little dogs that I passed on the street.

"What kind of dog is he?" and "This one, is he a mixture?"

I finally decided on a miniature poodle from a breeder of champions in Las Vegas, Nevada. His sister, the white poodle, was going to Sweden to become a show dog.

I texted the yoga teacher who encouraged me to take the leap, "What should I name him?"

"Rama," she said, "Lord Rama, after the Hindu God."

The day finally came to pick up Rama at the United Airlines cargo area. David and I were on line with our papers when a small cage arrived.

David said intuitively, "That's him." I kneeled down to the cage and peeked between the bars. A very small quiet black furry animal looked at me and we tongue kissed. "I can't believe he's mine," I sniffled.

After we presented our papers, we opened the cage. I picked him up and held him. What a furry treasure!! Awwwwwww. I took him everywhere. Choir rehearsal, car rides, yoga practice, shopping. He never made a sound. One day, he found his voice, and had to stay home.

Every morning I'd walk him to the beach and took photos with tourists. I smiled proudly and happily at everyone we passed. He said hello to all the strangers on the street, no matter how strange they seemed. He had homeless people laughing. He jumped on everyone and most people loved it and said,

"What a happy puppy!"

"I wish I were that happy."

He wanted to play with all the dogs on our path but he kept punching them in the face with his paws and most of them growled, but there was one dog his size. They punched each other and that worked for them. We met up with Charlie a few times until his owner and I exchanged phone numbers. He'd text me most mornings.

159

"Is 9:00 ok?"

"How's 8:45 today?"

"Yes, yes and yes."

Charlie's owner had taken the off-the-leash training course so we could let them loose, and off they ran. Rama, enamored with Charlie's behind, always followed. When the owner called "Charlie," Rama was there too. But it was time to get him fixed. Now they would run neck and neck and roll in the grass biting each other, happy as clams. I rushed to the meeting point each morning, and, as soon as I spotted Charlie and his master, I let go of the leash and off they flew into each others arms like long lost lovers.

One morning three other dogs joined and a lady holding her white female foufou yelled out joyfully, "Look at this, it's a dog party."

I tried to get a photo of him for my holiday cards, but no way would he sit long enough to take a picture. I called my dog trainer and she came equipped with a long leash, treats and a sit command with sound effects. Rama smiled for each photo. The regal one, with his arms folded, was the winning shot.

One day, Rama introduced me to a neighbor, Jude, while she was walking her dog, Otto. The dogs had a so-so interaction. But Jude, with her Shakespearian, English accent, dramatic flair, and kindness, was multifaceted, multi-purposed and multitasked. She became the friend in the neighborhood for whom I had always looked, the artist who would re-create Marina's painting, and the one who connected me to Ellen.

Ellen Frazier-Jameson conducted a writing class where I got the support to write down the family stories to which Jude patiently listened.

Back to Rama, I emailed the great nieces about their new cousin. They can't wait to meet him and so they did, that summer. The family reunion meant everything to me and was the culmination of years of separation.

Left to Right: Ellen & Jude

Charlie & Rama

The cousins: Rocky and Rama

L-R: Mikey, Rocky, Rama, John (my nephew)

L-R: Jen, Eve, Mikey, Isabel, John, (my nephew) Susan, top Lexie

L-R: Jerry & Amy (my niece)   L-R: David, Susan, Melissa (Amy's daughter), Amy & Jerry

Rama's trainer,
Kristen Thompson

Lord Rama

Left to Right: Jude, Ellen & Susan

From left: Teofil and his army buddies, World War 1

32 MIKEY CARRIES THE BATON

Just when I thought that I hadn't heard much from the great nieces, except for a "Hi, want to say hello but we're so busy with school..." I got an email from Mikey their little brother, my 13 year old great nephew.

From: Michael Schneider
Subject: our family pictures
Date: March 22, 2017 at 6:02:25 PM EDT
To: Susan Rosler

Hello Aunt Susan
Recently Eve and I finished going through and naming all of the pictures that you gave to me. It was very interesting and I learned a lot about our family. However, there was one photo that Nani (Eve) could not identify. It looks like it takes place in World War I based on the uniforms and I think it might be Teofil but I'm not sure. Do you think you can tell me who the people in the picture are?

I called my sister and got her take of the photo reviews. She said, "Everyday he comes over with his iPad and wants to know the name of everyone in the picture, and, their connection to each other. He's driving me crazy. Why does he care about all those people?"

Hi Mikey,

The man on the far left is Teofil. The others are his army buddies.
Love, Aunt Susan

From: Michael Schneider
Subject: Teofil
Date: March 23, 2017
To: Susan Rosler

Hello Aunt Susan,
Thank you for responding to my email so fast. I have another question for you about Teofil. I would like to know how he is related to us. I know he is your great uncle but on your mom or dad's side and through which of your grandparents.

Hi Mikey,
Teofil is on my mother's side. My mother's mother, Berta, had a sister named, Pepi. Teofil is Pepi's husband. Teofil and Pepi had two children, Hedi and Kurt. Hedi is still alive in Israel. Kurt was married to Olga. Olga was in concentration camp and is in the story that Tuvia wrote. Tuvia, the son of Kurt and Olga, published Teofil's diary and is an amazing person living in Israel.
Love, Aunt Susan

Hi Mikey,
Did you read the book?
Love, Aunt Susan

From: Michael Schneider
Subject: " In the Line of Fire"
Date: March 23, 2017
To: Susan Rosler

Yes, I did read the book. I found it very fascinating. Teofil was a very interesting man and to think that man who served in the Austro-Hungarian army and fought on the Russian and Italian front during World War 1 is related to us, is crazy.
Love, Michael

From: Susan Rosler
Subject: Re: "In the Line of Fire"
Date: March 24, 2017
To: Michael Schneider

Hi Mikey,
It goes to show you the absurdity of all wars and that we are all connected. And, yes, isn't it all crazy & so much fun to look back at and see the connections. He was such an amazing, lovable, character, a real hero.
I am thrilled that you are interested in all this!!!!!Hugs to you. Keep asking questions. I thrive on the feedback.
Love, Aunt Susan

Subject: our family
March 24, 2017

Dear Aunt Susan,
I would love to know the stories of how everyone who was in Austria in our family escaped when the Nazis came in World War II and where they went. I know some parts of some of the stories but not the whole story.

love,
Michael

Dear Aunt Susan,
Thank you so much I am so happy you are going to tell me all of the stories. Once again Happy Birthday. **I think it is very important to keep the stories of past generations alive for the future generations.**

love,
Michael

I sent him all the emails of family history that I had communicated to his sisters earlier.

Hi Mikey,

The lady on the left is my grandmother. Pepi is her youngest sister. Pepi's husband, Teofil, the jokester, is standing behind her holding up the rabbit ears. The other man with the beard is my grandfather, Schimson.

We called him Grossvater (grandfather) and he lived with us when he came to America.

Love, Aunt Susan

Dear Aunt Susan,

Thank you so much for telling me all those stories I love them all. I do have some questions though. When Nani (your sister) was telling me about her grandmother she said her name was Sarah and you said it was Berta. Is this possibly a German translation? I would also like to know where she is buried because I have this photo of Schimson standing over her grave. I think it was very crazy what everyone had to go through to get out of Austria. Oh, and one more question. Who was older Nazl Froehlich or Mathius?

love, Michael

Hi Mikey,

    My grandmother died in Mauritius, an island off the coast of Madagascar. That is where the refugee camp was.

I was named after her.

My Hebrew name is Sara Bryna. I believe people called her Berta, maybe a nickname.

Nazl was the oldest brother.

Siggy next. **Mathias**, the youngest.

Nazl escaped to Switzerland with his wife and two children, Harry and Sonia. Sonia's children and grandchildren still live there. Harry and his wife, Inge, moved to the US and we saw them regularly.

Siggy was killed in a camp in Belgium with his wife and daughter.

Mathias went to England and was prosperous. His son is cousin Peter.

Nazl's son was Harry, as I said earlier.

Harry's son is Royce, who lives in Forest Hills, Queens.

Royce is a professional drummer, sound engineer and a PhD Jungian Psychotherapist.

I would love the opportunity to introduce you.

Love, Aunt Susan

left to right (counterclockwise) Rose, Fani, Mathius, Shimson (Grossvater), Siggy, Berta, Nazl

From: Susan Rosler
Subject: Family tree
Date: March 29, 2017
To: Mikey Schneider

Hi Mikey,

I found the family tree that Hedi wrote in the first version of Teofil's Diary, in which she put the name Berta for my grandmother.

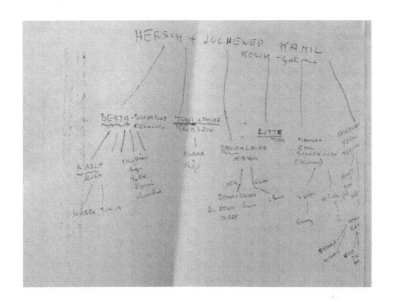

Dear Aunt Susan

Thank you for telling me all of this. It was a big mystery for me and Nani as to who was older Nazl or Mathius. And who Mathius's son was. I would love to meet these people. I love meeting family and mapping out the family tree and collecting all the stories.

 Love, Mikey

March 30, 2017
Hi Mikey,

It is so exciting for me to have someone involved and interested in the family history.

This means the world to me.♥♥♥♥

Dear Aunt Susan,

I love learning about my family history. It is all so interesting. I think you should write a book about all this history.

       Love,
        Mikey

Hi Mikey,

   Thank you, Mikey,
     Maybe, LOL

33 ROYCE AND THE DIARY

In June, 2014, I visited Israel and saw cousin Tuvia after 40 years. At that time he had shown me *Tagebuch Eines Juedischen Soldaten* which was the diary of Teofil, *A Soldier's Diary, WWl*.   He had given me the book about his father, Kurt. But the one that contained the authentic diary of his grandfather, Teofil, with amazing, black and white, period photos, was the incredible and fascinating one. This diary had survived the front lines of WW1 and the devastation of WW II. What was its route? How was its survival possible? What could I do to earn this book?

After this Israeli trip, David and I drove to N.Y. and Boston in August. There we made the usual rounds. We went to see: Alice, from the Lake House, now in Melbourne, Florida. Cousin Sonia, Rachella's daughter, in Baltimore. Maggie's cousin, Ida, N.Y., cousin Madey, Long Island, Gladys in the Boston area and finally cousin Royce in Queens, N.Y. Royce is the son of Harry, who is the son of Nazl, my mother's oldest brother. Yes, I'm keeping track.

Royce, David and I were having dinner out.

"Royce, it was so exciting to see cousin Tuvia in Israel after all those years. He showed me a beautiful hard-cover book with WW1 photos that he had self-published of the diary of a soldier in WW I."

Royce said, "*Tagebuch eines Juedishen Soldaten*...I know the book."

"No, you can't know this one. It must be another with a similar name. There were only a few copies made."

We returned to Royce's home for coffee and cake.   Suddenly, Royce produced the book with a smile,

"Is this the book?" My jaw dropped in amazement,

"That's the book. How did you get this?"

"Do you want the book?"

"No, no, I can't take it from you."

He asked Jerry, his best friend, who had joined us,

"Did you ever see this book?"

"No."

"Do you think I could manage without it?"

"Yep"

I waited in the background, eyes wide open and salivating.

"Take the book," he said.

"Really, wowww!" and of course, we took photos of the moment.

At home, I opened the book and found a family tree and a note from Hedi to Fani and Harry and it was clear how Royce inherited this treasure that he chose to pass it on to me. Thank you, Maggie and the universe for bringing it all to light.

David, Susan, Royce

Four generations: From left to right
Grossvater, Harry, Royce(baby), Nazl

From l-r: Inge (Harry's wife),
Grossvater, Harry, Royce, Nazl,
Fani

On Apr 12, 2017, Susan Rosler wrote:

Hi Mikey,
    Did the yoga mat arrive?
Love. Aunt Susan

Hi Aunt Susan,
    Yes, I just got the yoga mat
I love it so much. Thank you.
Xoxoxo

On Apr 13, 2017, Susan Rosler wrote:
Hi Mikey

    This is the link to my favorite yoga video. Follow this and save it. **Yoga is the most important message I have.**

Love, Aunt Susan

https://www.youtube.com/watch?v=VNt9qP0_hYI
Ali Macgraw: Mind, Body & Spirt

From: Michael Schneider
Subject: Re: ali macgraw /mind body spirit
Date: April 13, 2017 at 10:18:02 PM EDT
To: Aunt Susan Rosler

Hello Aunt Susan,
    Thank you so much for the mat and the DVD. I love yoga.
It looks like I have found a new hobby.
              Love, Mikey

34 TERI DESARIO, Giving Voice

On Apr 8, 2017

Hi Mikey,

I sent you a book called *I Will Plant You a Lilac Tree*. My voice teacher and friend, Teri DeSario, recommended it to me. Teri met the author, Laura Hillman, by chance at a phone booth in London. Teri's compassion sparked a mystical connection between the two women. They hugged and cried their hearts out as Laura told of her horrific experience in concentration camps. Shortly after that encounter the book was written. That same teacher, Teri DeSario, encouraged me to write down my family stories and that's how it all got started.

By the way, Teri had two hit records years back (in the 70's): "Yes, I'm Ready" and "Ain't Nothing Gonna Keep Me from You."

The book was VERY amazing. Let me know what you think of it.

Much love, Aunt Susan

Center- Susan & Teri DeSario

Teri DeSario

Hello Aunt Susan,

Thank you so much. The book sounds so fascinating I love reading, especially, a book like that. I cannot wait to get it.

love, Mikey

April 14, 2017

Hello Aunt Susan,

I finished the book, *I Will Plant You a Lilac Tree.* It was one of the best books I have ever read. It was amazing. Now it is my turn to recommend a book to you. The book, *Irena's Children,* is a book about a woman named Irene Sendler. She was a Christian woman, who, during World War II helped 2,500 kids escape from the Warsaw ghetto. It is an entirely true story about the female Schindler, as she is known as. It is a truly action and adventure packed novel.

Hi Mikey,   **April 14, 2017**

Yes. I saw the movie version.
It was totally incredible. She was such an awesome heroine. We are interested in the same stories.
Love, Aunt Susan

178

35 RACHELLA, Sharing with Love and Delight in Her Heart

April 15, 2017
Hi Mikey,
  Below is the story of my father's first cousin, Rachella.

  My father totally revered his cousin, Rachella, a concentration camp survivor. Every now and then, he would take me with him on an Amtrak excursion from New York to Baltimore. My mother would pack a brown bag with lunch and a change of clothes. Rachella's husband, Paul, was a tailor and her two children were Henry and Sonia.
  These visits with my father were such a treat. Rachella was smiley, warm, friendly and always so happy to see us. She loved to chat with me and was interested in anything I had to say.
  My family was invited to Henry's Bar Mitzvoh and I asked if I could bring a boyfriend. She immediately said yes. She didn't ask how long I knew him, if he was serious, or what he did for a living.
  Through the years, I watched her children grow up and have children of their own. Henry had two, and Sonia had six. As an adult, I visited on my own. Anytime I asked if I could come, was a good time. Pickled herring, chicken soup and rye bread were always there.
  In the evenings, the large dining room table was surrounded by children, grandchildren and guests. Warmth, hominess and love were forever present around the oval table of clanging plates, happy chatter, and delicious aromas.
  In Rachella's Polish accent and charming manner she would say, "The door is always open," or "Stand up straight, you don't owe nobody money."
  One day I asked about the concentration camp.
She explained:
  "I had to hold on to a piece of bread in my smock and keep it hidden all day. My mother, father, and brother disappeared from the beginning. I always wondered why I was chosen to be a worker and not my brother."
  "You know," she said with a chuckle,
  "I was in a tough spot. I was already 27, skinny, a little diseased, no hair do and no men in the compound. How would I ever get married?"
  Lo and behold, "After the liberation, what was left of us was gathered outside the camp. A man from my hometown recognized me. His wife and children were killed. So, he was available. Paul was a very good man, short, but a really good man." She showed a photo and yes, he was more than a head shorter than her.

Rachella had many photos of all the people she had known and explained her connection to them with total love and delight in her heart. Whenever I visited, she would make arrangements with whatever grandchildren were around and create a happening.

Sonia, her daughter, to this day, continues her legacy.

Rachella

From Left to Right: David, Henry, Susan, Rachella, Sonia

Susan and Cousin Sonia, Rachella's daughter

Hi Aunt Susan,

Wow, what a beautiful story when I was showing Nani (Eve) the pictures you gave me she identified Henry and Rachella but she didn't know how we were related to them now I know she was your father's cousin. She sounds like such a strong amazing woman. Thanks for sharing the story.

Love you, Mikey

p.s. Happy Passover and Easter. xoxoxo

Hello Aunt Susan,

Do you know the names and maybe birthdates of your father's parents. Thanks. I'm trying to grow my family tree.   Love you, Mikey

April 21, 2017

Hi Mikey,

His mother's name was Marie and his father was Louis.

Love, Aunt Susan

Hi Aunt Susan,

Thank you so much for giving me this info. This really helps me with my family tree.

Love you ♥ Mikey

Hi Mikey

Here is a family tree, of my father's side, given to me by Barrie, cousin Madey's daughter. Barrie created this tree for a college project. The information was given to her by her grandmother, Thelma.

PATERNAL FAMILY TREE

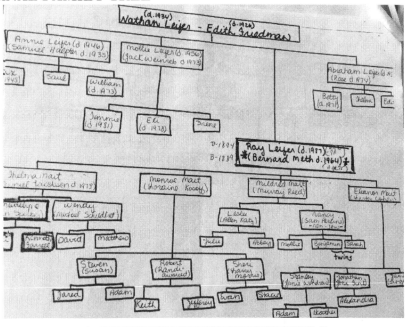

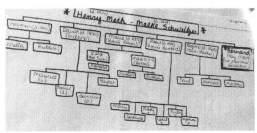

36 COUSIN COURTNEY, Author of *The Number on Her Arm*

From: Susan Rosler
Subject: LISTEN UP
Date: April 22, 2017 at 3:15:07 PM EDT
To: Mikey Schneider

Hi Mikey,
    You will be getting a **signed** book from Courtney Tisch. Courtney is the daughter of my first cousin Ron, Elsie's son. Elsie was my father's sister.

It seems that Courtney wrote a book called *The Number on Her Arm.*

It is about her grandmother, (Ron's wife's mother) who survived her experience in Auschwitz.

    I heard about the book from cousin Henry, Rachella's son, a while ago. I decided to look it up, due to your interest and also mine. Per chance, I couldn't find a copy on line so I dared to email Ron's wife, Eddi, to ask how I could buy a copy.
    I then learned that the book was in all the Holocaust museums and Courtney had been invited to speak on it several times, in Washington DC, also in Toronto. She received a monetary award for the book and much fame in certain circles. Below is what I copied from the Internet.

Courtney Tisch is a writer and educator from Washington, DC. After spending several years after college trying to be an actor as well as working at various non-profit organizations, Courtney decided to go back to school in 2012 for her Masters of Education from The George Washington University. The manuscript for The Number on Her Arm was first written during a Children's Literature course she took in her final semester of graduate school in 2013. The book eventually went on to become a John Horrworth Children's Book Award winner. Courtney ultimately became motivated to pursue publication of this book due to the strength, endurance, and selflessness of her grandparents who were both Holocaust survivors. It is her hope that this book will not only let the memory of her grandparents live on forever, but that it will also serve to educate children from all over the world about the Holocaust.

    I had seen Courtney only once when she was a child.

As a result of this reconnection, Courtney, her mother, Eddi, and I have rekindled our relationship.
Love, Aunt Susan

My first cousin, Ron, and Courtney

Aunt Elsie and Ron

Susan & cousin Ron

Hi Aunt Susan,

Wow this book seems like it's going to be awesome like the last one, and this one is written and signed by a relative of ours. Wow how amazing!!! Thank you Aunt Susan, this really means a lot to me.

Love Mikey

On Apr 29, 2017, Michael Schneider wrote:

Hello Eddi.

I am the grandnephew of Susan Rosler. My name is Michael Schneider. I would like to say that the book was amazing. The message behind it was stunning and I loved the way it was communicated through a kids' book. I think the message of the book should be spread especially among kids. You should be very proud of your daughter, Courtney, and your parents.

Love,
Michael Schneider

37 INVITATION FROM TUVIA

Hi Mikey,

The email below came from Tuvia. It's an invitation to his daughter's wedding. He is inviting all family and people connected to family so that he can create a reunion as well. Can you make it? Love, Aunt Susan

To our family around the world,
On July 13th, 2017, our youngest daughter, Lilach, is getting married. The wedding will be held in Caesarea, Israel.
Anyone who is planning (or wanting) to visit Israel around that time is invited to the wedding (an opportunity for an international family gathering).
Liora and Tuvia Erez (Reiss)   Israel

Hi Aunt Susan,

I will have to ask my parents. Thank you so much for inviting me. What area of Israel is it in do you know?

Love you, Mikey

Hi Mikey,

I hope you are considering the trip to Israel. It is the chance of a lifetime. Hedi, the daughter of Teofil, is about 90 or more and you would get to meet and interview her. According to the story she told me, she was put on a ship to Palestine by Fani at the age of 13 and made it there to have children and grandchildren. There are very few people left in our family or anywhere that are still around that escaped and were old enough to remember their experience. There is another woman, also named Hedi, the daughter of Uncle David, that is also still around in Israel. The offspring of these people are the "sabras" that founded Israel, had to fight for its survival, and keep it going.

We could travel around, see the sights, and visit the relatives. A trip to remember forever! You can write your own book before you're 15. lol And it is SAFE.
Love, Susan

Hi aunt Susan,
my mother is 90% ok with going with me and she wants to know what airline you are flying and when are you going to leave.
love you xoxoxo   Mikey

38 **ISRAELI COUSIN HANNA**, Seize the Opportunity

Hi Mikey,

I'm sending you a little story to begin introducing you to the Israeli cousins.

One day my friend Gladys said, "My brother-in-law asked if I wanted to go on a tour around Israel. What do you think, Susan, should I go?"

I answered, "Yes of course, why not seize the opportunity?" and, I jumped in, "Can I go with you?"

We packed up and got ready for the tour in the summer of 2008.

When we arrived at the hotel, I called cousin Hedi, who had been to America several times and introduced me to Israel. She would send colorful calendars of Israeli life, and photos of her daughters, Hanna and Raya. These 'sabras' (native of Israel) were legend-like to me, especially since I had never met them.

Hedi said, "Call my daughter, Hanna."

Hanna asked, "What is the name of your tour?"

I answered and she said, "Ok, fine, I'll contact you."

The tour bus moved around taking us from place to place.

When we were close to Caesarea, the bus driver called me forward, "Stand by the front door exit."

He stopped the bus, and a beautiful tall sabra with perfect posture in boots and khaki pants was standing at the stop.

The driver announced, as in a movie scene, "This is your cousin Hanna."

Totally blown away, I got off the bus quivering and speechless, and gave her a big hug.

She said, "Let me take you to lunch, show you around and bring you to my home."

The house was beautifully decorated and filled with paintings she had done. Surrounding the house, was an amazing garden of fruit trees that she and her husband had planted.

I figured out that she and the bus driver had planned the dramatic surprise, well worth the effort. I'm sure I was sorely missed that day by the jealous tour passengers who were left with their tongues hanging out.

Hanna and her husband, Yacov

Re: Hanna and the bus driver
Date: May 2, 2017
To: Aunt Susan Rosler

I love it. All your stories are fantastic. They bring a moment in time to life again. They let you see what the people in it saw. I wonder what the other people on the bus were thinking.

love you, Mikey

1912 photo - Counterclockwise from left - My Great Grandfather (Hersch), Nazl, Berta, Siggy (baby), Great Grandmother (Jochewed), Toni, Minna, David, Pepi, my Grandfather (Schimson), Lotte

My mother was not yet born.

39 COUSIN SYLVIA

May 3, 2017

Hi Mikey,

Here is the story of cousin Sylvia.

Sylvia lived in Birmingham, England. Her mother, Klara, escaped from Vienna and was the daughter of Toni, one of my grandmother's sisters in the 1912 photo.

I emailed Sylvia to get more information.

"Sylvia, what happened to Toni?"

"Unfortunately, she and my grandfather were picked up   in Yugoslavia and ended up in Auschwitz."

"How did your parents escape?"

"My mother got a 'job as a housemaid' in England which was a trick used to save some Jewish women. I find it hard to believe that my parents were brave and clever enough to put Ditta [Sylvia's older sister] on the 'Kindertransport' (Children transport) and get out of the country themselves."

Nevertheless, cousin Sylvia, was a barrel of fun, and, when she came to the U.S. for a summer, we travelled together across the country from New York to California.

I had visited her in Birmingham, England and when she spent a year in Jerusalem, I met up with her there. It was in Jerusalem that she met Simon from Glasgow, Scotland.

The pair returned to the UK and a year later got married. Sylvia is very kind, loving and quite clever. Years later, she and Simon sold their mock Tudor house, gathered up Sylvia's 90 year old, mother, Klara, and immigrated to Jerusalem. They made "Aliyah" (moved to Israel) and joined their three children that had done this a few years before: each, after completing their respective university studies.

Sylvia is a Sabbath observer and has many grandchildren. Her free time is spent being a role model to her grandchildren and steadily participating in lots of charitable endeavors.

Sylvia and Susan

From L-R: Gideon, Sylvia, Sarah

Kindertransport:
The parents, in desperate attempts to save their children, gave them to an organization of strangers, with the understanding that if the parent survived, the children would be returned to them. Some of the children were very well cared for, others were abused and some foster parents fought legal battles to keep the child. Ditta, Sylvia's sister, was one of these children. It took years for the parents to finally get custody of their child.

40 COUSIN EDNA, Synchronicities, the Magic of the Spirit

May 4, 2017
Hi Mikey,
Here comes another cousin.
Love, Aunt Susan

Edna lives in Ramat Gan and is the daughter of "Rote"
(redheaded) Hedi, whose father was David, another sibling in the 1912 photo.

When Edna was in her early 20's, young and beautiful, she and a friend visited the set of the filming of "Exodus" hoping to be an extra. As luck would have it, Otto Preminger was so impressed with Edna that he created a special speaking part for her. "Hello my name is Edna. Let me show you around the Kibbutz." In addition, he offered her a movie contract.

Her mother said, "No way will you live the life style of an actress. You need to get married and have children."

So Edna became a flight attendant, married the handsome star pilot, Zvika, and had three children: Gal, Ravit and Shiri. Edna is devoted to her grandchildren and is a fabulous cook.

Zvika was in the air force during the 1967 war and was on the team that destroyed 300 enemy planes in the airport before they left the ground causing the war to end in six days.

After his military duty was over, he was on reserve. Since he flew El Al, he made many trips to New York and occasionally we got together in Manhattan.

One time I was home watching the news. War broke out in Lebanon in 1982 and there on the TV screen were the planes. I thought, OMG, Zvika. Something in the atmosphere made me go out and stop at the local Lamston's chain store. At that precise moment of the day, Zvika was at the cashier with Ravit and Shiri.

"Zvika, is that you?? Aren't you in the war?"

"Yes, but only during the week, on weekends, I fly El Al."

This kind of synchronicity happens to me regularly. I may not have seen someone for several years, but if they're in the area from across the world, something gets me out there and we connect. It's the magic of the spirit.

Edna   Zvika

On May 4, 2017, Michael Schneider wrote:

Wow these people sound amazing. I remember reading about David in the *Line of Fire* book. It is crazy how you always connect with these people even if you don't plan on it. That is crazy how she was going to get a full speaking part in a movie.

Love Mikey

Hi Mikey,

An email from Zvika came to my mailbox earlier today, just hours before I was about to send you the story of Edna
and Zvika. In addition, I received a telemarketing call from Israel. What a coincidence.

Love, Susan

41 **Tante Minna,** Don't Be Angry, Laugh It Off

Hi Mikey,
More cousins

Tante Minna had two boys, Walter and Erich. Walter and his wife, Ruth, also had two sons, Ami and Danny. During my visit to Israel, the military had Family Day and Walter, a Lieutenant Commander of the Navy, honored me by showing me the inside of a submarine. I was very impressed with how cutely things were organized in little compartments and so much could fit inside.

I was also Zvika's guest and got to ride with him in a two seater Piper plane. I smuggled my camera aboard in a paper bag and was able to take one photo of his back before getting airsick.

Erich, the other son of Tante Minna, moved to California with his wife, Annie, and sons Ilan and Ron. Ilan was a great scholar and became a prosperous world traveler, and when I visited Annie, Erich and Ron, she was such a sweetheart that she gave me an outstanding necklace and matching earrings from her costume jewelry collection. We shared our sewing interest and had much to discuss. After using her sewing machine, however, I accidentally took her bobbin. Of course, I mailed it back, but, instead of being angry, she laughingly joked about it for years.

Counterclockwise, from left: Tante Minna, Berta (my grandmother), Tante
Pepi, Aunt Rose (my mother's sister), Grossvater, Teofil, Aunt Fani

Walter Shanon

left to right- Dubi, Walter, Susan, Ami, Ruth, Danny

Erich, Annie and Ron in L.A.   Ilan Shanon & his wife, Eileen

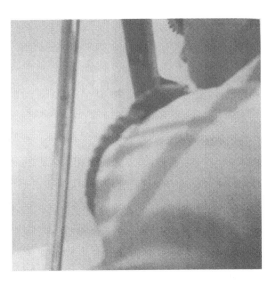

Zvika in the piper plane. Photo taken by me with smuggled camera.

42 FORGIVENESS, Letting Go and Inviting In

My sister had been angry with me for years, which kept me from seeing her grandchildren.

Fueled by Gladys's steam when she said, "Find those great nieces," I dared to ask for their emails and searched for the right spark to illuminate their interest.

I tried an old family photo, nothing. I sent a picture of my mom, who was a goddess to me and everyone else. I got a thank you, but no bite. They didn't really know who this woman was.

Was it a coincidence that, just in time, Tuvia sent that beautifully written article of his mother, Olga? It was such a good story that the wheels began to turn and the weave of the web was forming.

I started the tale of my family's exodus from Vienna, and waited.

But, as Royce said, "They're not going to care until Eve, their own grandmother, shows up"

And so they did. It has been smooth sailing ever since.

Just got this email from Mikey:

From: Michael Schneider
Subject: recipes
Date: May 14, 2017 at 4:02:13 PM EDT
To: Aunt Susan Rosler

Hello Aunt Susan,

Recently I have started cooking a lot for fun and for dinner. When Nani saw that I was cooking she told me tales of your mother, Charlotte, cooking everything from candy to birthday cakes to Austrian cuisine, like strudel and wiener schnitzel. She also told me she had a recipe box with all of her recipes in them. I was wondering if you have some of those recipes or know where they are.
love you, Mikey

I looked for my mother's Viennese cookbook on my shelf, got the name and author, found a copy on the internet, bought it, and sent it to Mikey. I then took the cappuccino that David lovingly prepared for me and sipped it on my peaceful terrace. From the corner of my eye, I could see my mother laughing and joining me to appreciate the moment.

All was forgiven between Eve and me and now I can testify, there are huge benefits to forgiveness!!!!!

Mikey and the Viennese cookbook

43 IN CONCLUSION Yoga Keeps You Young

Hi Mikey,

Try this:

Put on your video, you tube or DVD and get on your mat. Breathe deeply, in and out, through your nose, mouth closed. Think of someone or something that you are grateful for and smile. Focus on your breath and think only of the breath. Other thoughts will come in, but remind yourself to ignore them and go back to the breath. It's hard to keep out all thoughts. Strive to keep your mind free of all petty annoyances. It is a practice, a discipline, and little by little, it gets better. Follow the poses. Some seem difficult at first, but you will improve step by step. It is not a competitive sport. You don't have to be as adept as the model in the video or the person next to you. Each one has his or her, own path. No one is judging you and be sure not to judge yourself. You don't have to do all the poses. Whenever something seems too difficult, go into resting pose and just keep breathing.

The health benefits of a regular yoga practice are infinite. Yoga gives you better flexibility, posture, balance, respiration, digestion, immunity, circulation and memory.   It lowers cholesterol, blood sugar, blood pressure, and sodium levels. It gives you a healthy heart, relieves pain, controls arthritis, sciatica, Parkinson's, fibromyalgia and even Lyme disease. It also prevents osteoporosis and protects the spine. One of my yoga teachers said, "You are as young as your spine." In other word, the more flexible your spine, the younger you are.

The rest of the day is a reflection of what happens on the yoga mat. As you go about your day, avoid thinking of the past or the future. Stay in the present, focused on what you are doing. Whenever you feel discouraged, find gratitude. That is, think of things for which you are grateful. And, don't forget to smile. You are the director of your movie and in charge of the screenplay of your mind. So, fill up your mind space with good stuff. Bear no grudges in order to keep the playing field free of conflict. If something good happens, make a fuss. If something bad happens, don't focus or dwell on it. We are but a tiny speck in this vast universe. All the little things that we *think* are important, are *not*. None of it really matters. Our purpose is simply to be **happy**.

Yogis believe that life is eternal. The soul goes on. As Suzanne once said, "You can gag me, tie me up, lock me in a closet, and throw away the key, but you can't take away my soul."

I can see Maggie in her elegant high heels, hand on her hip, wink in her eye and pride in her heart. Thank you, Maggie, for a job well done. I connected with Mikey and the beautiful people reading this. We are all connected. We are all one, for no one has left this earthly plane. Their soul is always present and part of the atmosphere.

Breathe in the spirit of your loved ones breathe out. Breathe in again, breathe out and release, let it go, let it all go.

Thank you, God.

ACKNOWLEDGEMENTS

1. Writing Consultants

> Jude Perry****
> Ellen Frazer-Jameson
> Rosemary Ravinal
> Jeanne Mockridge
> Karen Mobilia
> Willa Kaufman
> Hanny Stadelmann
> Royce Froehlich
> Diane Choquette
> Al Serrano
> Rachel Davis
> Jacqueline Dorsey
> Daniel Bourgoin

2. Choir Family at Unity on the Bay

> Dale Stine, Choir Director
> Anthony Alvarez, Assistant
> Mayra Alvarez, Assistant
> Chris Jackson, CEO
> Juan del Hierro, Assistant

3. Yoga studios

> Green Monkey, Miami Beach
> Tropical Vinyasa, Miami Beach

4. Yoga Teachers
>Paul Toliuszis
>Ewa Josefsson
>Amy Litt Rabin
>Paula Walker
>Carlos Tao
>Jason Lawner
>Beth Ogden

5. Voice Teachers
>Teri DeSario
>Chris Arroyo
>Ariel Remos

6. Rama's Trainer
>Kristen Thompson

7. Rama's Breeder
>Ash's Mystical Poodles
>www.mysticalpoodles.com

8. Apple Store, Lincoln Road

9. Photos by Susan Rosler unless credited or photographer unknown.

10. David, of course

21936981R00111

Made in the USA
Columbia, SC
23 July 2018